Hermann Conring's

New Discourse on the Roman-German Emperor

Medieval and Renaissance Texts and Studies

Volume 282

In The Series:
Neo-Latin Texts and Translations

Hermann Conring's

New Discourse on the Roman-German Emperor

*Edited and translated
by*
Constantin Fasolt

Arizona Center for Medieval and Renaissance Studies
Tempe, Arizona
2005

Generous grants from the University of Chicago and Pegasus Limited for the Promotion of Neo-Latin Studies have assisted with meeting the publication costs of this volume.

© Copyright 2005
Arizona Board of Regents for Arizona State University

Library of Congress Cataloging-in-Publication Data

Conring, Hermann, 1606–1681.
 [Discursus novus de Imperatore Romano-Germanico. English]
 Hermann Conring's New discourse on the Roman-German Emperor / edited and translated by Constantin Fasolt.
   p. cm. — (Medieval and Renaissance texts and studies ; v. 282. Neo-Latin texts and translations)
 Includes bibliographical references.
 ISBN-13: 978-0-86698-325-9 (alk. paper)
  1. Holy Roman Empire — Early works to 1800. 2. Church and state — Early works to 1800. 3. Constitutional history — Holy Roman Empire — Early works to 1800. I. Fasolt, Constantin, 1951–. II. Title. III. Title: New discourse on the Roman-German Emperor. IV. Series: Medieval & Renaissance Texts & Studies (Series) ; v. 282.

JN3249.C613 2005
943'.02—dc22   2005020663

∞
This book is made to last.
It is set in Adobe Caslon Pro,
smyth-sewn and printed on acid-free paper
to library specifications.
Printed in the United States of America

Contents

Acknowledgments	vii
Introduction	ix
Chronology	xvii
Notes on the English Translation	xxiii
Notes on the Latin Text	xxxiii
Abbreviations	xxxvii

Discursus novus de imperatore Romano-Germanico	2
New Discourse on the Roman-German Emperor	3
A. The issue	3
B. What was the extent of the Roman empire in antiquity?	3
B.a. The extent of the ancient Roman empire in fact	7
B.b. The extent of the ancient Roman empire in law	11
C. What happened to the Roman empire from antiquity until the times of Charlemagne?	11
C.a. How the Roman empire was dismantled during the early Middle Ages	13
C.a.i. From Theodosius the Great to Charlemagne	13
C.a.ii. The special case of Italy	19
C.a.iii. The Roman empire at the time of Charlemagne's imperial coronation	29
C.b. The meaning of Charlemagne's imperial title	29
C.b.i. It did not apply to all of Italy or the eastern empire	31
C.b.ii. It did apply to Rome and the papacy	33
D. Were Germany and Italy ever absorbed into the Roman empire?	39
D.a. Germany, Italy, and the empire from Charlemagne to Otto the Great	41
D.a.i. Charlemagne	41
D.a.ii. Louis the Pious	43
D.a.iii. The later Carolingians	43
D.a.iv. Henry the Fowler and Otto the Great	47

D.b. Otto the Great's reorganization of the empire	53
D.b.i. The assemblies of Germany and Italy	53
D.b.ii. The German, Italian, and imperial crowns	55
D.b.iii. The election of the emperor	57
D.c. First conclusion: The emperor has no right to rule Germany and Italy	59
D.c.i. Objections from the common usage of the term "Roman empire"	59
D.c.ii. Objections from the titles used by the kings of Germany and Italy	61
D.c.iii. Germany is a separate state from the Roman empire and not subject to Roman law	63
D.d. Second conclusion: The papacy has no right to interfere in the affairs of Germany	63
D.d.i. Objections from the papacy's right to elect the emperor	63
D.d.ii. Objections from the papacy's right to transfer the empire to other rulers	63
D.d.iii. The insignificance of the role of the papacy	65
E. Does the Roman empire still exist today?	65
E.a. The extent of imperial power from Charlemagne to the present	67
E.a.i. From Charlemagne to Otto the Great	67
E.a.ii. From Otto the Great to Henry IV	71
E.a.iii. From Pope Gregory VII to the present	73
E.b. Third conclusion: The Roman empire has either ceased to exist completely or it is in the hands of the papacy	75
E.b.i. Objections from the Bible	77
E.b.ii. Objections from Roman law	79
E.b.iii. Objections from the dignity of the emperor	81
Corollaries	83
Guide to Further Reading	85
Works Cited in the *New Discourse*	95
Index	103

Acknowledgments

I would like to thank the University of Chicago, the American Philosophical Society, the John Simon Guggenheim Memorial Foundation, the National Humanities Center, the Gladys Krieble Delmas Foundation, the Max-Planck-Institut für Europäische Rechtsgeschichte, and the Herzog August Bibliothek in Wolfenbüttel for supporting the research of which this book is a result. For gracious permission to reproduce some material from my article "Author and Authenticity in Conring's *New Discourse on the Roman-German Emperor*: A Seventeenth-Century Case Study," *Renaissance Quarterly* 54 (2001): 188–220, I am grateful to the Renaissance Society of America. Special thanks are due to the College of the University of Chicago and its Dean, John Boyer, for assisting the publication of this volume with a subvention. I am grateful to Robert Bjork for giving this volume the imprimatur of MRTS, and to two anonymous readers for their constructive suggestions. I would also like to thank Leslie MacCoull for her proficient copyediting and Roy Rukkila for his relaxed management of the production process.

Introduction

Hermann Conring (1606–1681) is slowly gaining recognition as one of the few great thinkers on matters of history, politics, and law in seventeenth-century Germany. He deserves it. He clarified the history of German law as no one else had done before. His grasp of the inner workings of the Holy Roman Empire was superb, and his ability to expound it to his contemporaries unparalleled. His dream of short, clear, and systematic legal codes enacted for the common good by sovereign legislation was at least a century ahead of its time. He wished to turn the study of politics into an abstract science, but he also was convinced that science requires sound empirical foundations. He gathered as much information as he could about geography, population, commerce, industry, and society from all over Europe and the world. His lectures on the states of Europe led the way towards the development of statistics as a new social-scientific discipline that would become a reality in the eighteenth century. At the same time he was determined not to let the study of politics degenerate into mere data collection. In his main work of theory, *On Civil Prudence*, he sought to articulate the principles that governed politics as such, as an autonomous sphere of thought and action distinct from religion, morality, and jurisprudence.[1] He knew that after Machiavelli there was no turning back. In short, he emancipated politics from traditional authority and endowed its study with the dignity of science. Pufendorf (1632–1694), a generation younger than Conring and much better known, regarded him as more radical, more theoretical, and better informed about politics than his contemporaries. Pufendorf had it right.[2]

Conring had not meant to study politics. He was trained as a physician at the University of Leiden in the 1620s and he spent the 1630s and 1640s teaching natural philosophy and medicine at the University of Helmstedt. First and

---

[1] Hermann Conring, *De civili prudentia liber unus* (Helmstedt: H. Müller, 1662), reprinted in Hermann Conring, *Opera*, ed. Johann Wilhelm Goebel, 7 vols. (Brunswick: Meyer, 1730; repr. Aalen: Scientia, 1970–1973), 3:280–421. Henceforth I will refer to Goebel's edition of Conring's works as *Opera*.

[2] For Pufendorf's judgment see *Opera*, 1:xxvi. For more information about the scholarship, see the guide to further reading below, p. 87.

foremost he was a man of science. He was excited by the possibilities of scientific observation and committed to the task of healing. He conducted experiments to verify Harvey's new theory about the circulation of the blood and published a series of significant (though now almost entirely forgotten) books about such things as body temperature and the ideas of Paracelsus (which he detested). He supervised a plethora of medical dissertations, treated patients, and remained true to his medical calling until the end of his life.

Yet as early as his return to Germany from the Netherlands in 1631 his interests turned in a new direction. In part this was an accident, prompted by a chance encounter with Jacob Lampadius (1593–1649) that turned into an unexpectedly close friendship. Lampadius, a law professor in the employ of the dukes of Brunswick-Wolfenbüttel at the University of Helmstedt and soon to be a leading representative of the Protestant side in the negotiations leading up to the Peace of Westphalia, opened Conring's eyes to the importance of history. He had written an important book that Conring was going to use as the foundation for his lectures on the Holy Roman Empire for many years to come.[3] But Conring's conversations with Lampadius were able to change the course of his intellectual life only because of a reason more basic than chance: Conring's intense desire to help a people torn apart by war. As he put it about forty years later in one of his more important autobiographical statements, "what led me to teach courses on this subject over and over again were my desire to help our youth and my love of the public good."[4]

The first half of the seventeenth century, it needs to be remembered, witnessed the greatest calamity in German history until the twentieth century changed the scale on which calamities are weighed. Confessional unity was irreparably broken, Catholics and Protestants were fighting each other to the death, and Germany was being ground to destruction between the armies of Sweden and France. How was peace to be restored? For decades no one seemed to have an answer. It was enough to make you despair—and the despair is palpable in Conring's writings from the 1630s. Medicine helped a little. Never mind how deeply confused an age may be about questions of right and wrong, there is a satisfaction in helping

---

[3] Jacob Lampadius, *De iurisdictione, iuribus principum et statuum imperii* (Heidelberg: Geyder, 1620). Conring renamed it *Tractatus de republica Romano-Germanica* and *Tractatus de constitutione imperii Romano-Germanici*. He had it reprinted in 1634, in 1642, and with his own extensive commentary in 1671.

[4] "Frequenter enim repetere illam institutionem, studium iuvandae nostrae adolescentiae et commodi publici amor me adegit": *Opera*, 2:25–26, quoted from the preface to Conring's commentary on Lampadius, *De republica Romano-Germanica*, ed. Hermann Conring (Helmstedt: H. Müller, 1671; repr. in *Opera*, 2:22–237).

the sick that transcends all moral or religious uncertainty. But medicine dealt with the body physical. It offered no cure for the body politic.

History did. Or so Conring was persuaded by the reading Lampadius encouraged him to undertake. For Germans had a definite view of their own past. They thought that they were living in the Roman empire—the same Roman empire that had been founded by Augustus at the birth of Christ and that had been prophesied to endure until the end of time. They believed that their own king was none other than the Roman emperor himself. Even Lampadius still began his book with the founding of Rome. But this, so Conring came to be convinced, was profoundly wrong. Germany had always been a sovereign independent state with its own history and law, quite separate from Rome. In fact, the kings of Germany ruled on constitutional foundations that had nothing to do with ancient Rome at all. Germans were living in Germany, not Rome. Their past was German, not Roman, and their commonwealth was founded in the early Middle Ages, not when Romulus built his city.

That Germany was constantly confused with Rome was, of course, a habit of very ancient standing. But the habit was intellectually indefensible and politically downright dangerous. It claimed for the Roman emperor a right to rule the world that could only lead to war. No such right existed. A state, no matter whether it was Germany or Rome or any other state, was simply a community of people free to govern their own affairs as they saw fit—what Aristotle had once called a *polis*, what the Romans used to call a *civitas*, and what Conring liked to call a *respublica*, a commonwealth or state. Of course there were limits to political freedom. But those were the limits of nature and natural law, not Roman law or the rule of the Roman emperor. No state was universal. Those who maintained the opposite merely created pretexts for "starting wars, promoting turmoil, and overturning the state," as Conring was going to put it in chapter fifty-five of his *New Discourse on the Roman-German Emperor*.

In short, there was a simple explanation why the German body politic was sick: the German people were confused about their past. Because they were confused about their past, they were confused about the nature of their commonwealth. Because they were confused about the nature of their commonwealth, they went to war for the wrong reasons. And because they went to war for the wrong reasons, they could not find the road to peace. The logic was powerful and simple: bad history made peace impossible. Good history was required for the common good.

These insights must have come to Conring with the force of a revelation. They inspired him with a determination to set the record straight that would not flag for the remaining fifty years of his life. There were so many things that needed to be done, so many errors crying out for correction, so many truths to be established. Positive law had to be distinguished from natural law, and natural law had to be distinguished from international law. German law needed to be unearthed from the archives in which its history was languishing. Roman law needed to be placed in the historical distance where it belonged. The boundaries of Germany needed to be defined in order to avoid confusion about the question where Germany ended and where Rome, or France, or Poland began. The history of Germany needed to be written in order to describe how Germany and Rome had been related to each other over time. The geography, demography, economy, law, constitution, history, size, and culture of the commonwealth needed to be examined in empirical detail in order to determine whatever measures would improve its well-being, not only for Germany, but for any sovereign state. The young had to be taught how to advance the common good instead of undermining peace by ill-conceived respect for Rome's pretensions to universality. And so on.

The intelligence and range of these investigations earned Conring a European reputation. In 1650 Queen Christina of Sweden invited him to work for her in Stockholm. He visited, was tempted, but in the end declined. His lord, Duke August of Brunswick-Wolfenbüttel, rewarded him with a professorship in politics and a second salary, on top of his professorship and salary in medicine. He went on to teach politics and history to a generation of students at the University of Helmstedt. He also advised princes in and out of Germany on their affairs and was appointed privy counselor at more than one princely court. The kings of France, Denmark, and Sweden drew on his expertise—not to mention the dukes of Brunswick-Wolfenbüttel and the counts of his native East Frisia. Thanks to one of his students, Johann Christian von Boineburg (1622–1672), he had particularly close relations to the archbishop of Mainz, who played a major role in German politics during the generation after the Peace of Westphalia was concluded in 1648. The Habsburgs themselves looked favorably on at least some of his writings. He grew famous and wealthy. When he died at the age of seventy-five in 1681, he left a record of literally hundreds of publications, a sizeable estate, and a library of well over four-and-a-half thousand books. His political works are now largely forgotten, and his medical ones barely get an honorable mention in the annals of science. But his break with the universal claims of Roman law and his turn to history and sovereignty was one of the most unequivocal successes in German intellectual history.[5]

The *New Discourse on the Roman-German Emperor* was the first book to inform the public about Conring's view of the true nature of the relationship between

---

[5] Any reader familiar with early modern Europe will understand that Conring's ideas about history and law were not unprecedented. But Conring was the first to give these ideas a form that assured their acceptance in Germany. For more information, see the guide to further reading below, p. 87.

Germany and the Roman empire. It was published in 1642 in an unknown place, probably Leiden. It was also published against Conring's will. Technically speaking, the *New Discourse* was not even a book by Conring at all. Technically speaking, it was a pirated reprint of a dissertation published in 1641 by Bogislaus Otho von Hoym, one of Conring's students. This raises interesting questions about its authenticity. Those questions are too complicated to be treated here in detail.[6] But a few observations are in order to clarify the reasons why the *New Discourse* may nonetheless be considered good evidence for Conring's thought.

Seventeenth-century dissertations written at German universities are not to be confused with dissertations written by graduate students nowadays. Today, the written dissertation represents the culmination of a student's academic progress. It must embody the results of original research. Its approval and publication certify the student's admission to the guild of academic professionals. The defense is merely a stage on the way towards that goal.

In the seventeenth century it was the other way round. It was the oral defense that certified the student's successful completion of an academic course of studies. The written dissertation was merely a means towards that end. The defense took place in a public academic setting in which the student was required to demonstrate that he was able to maintain a certain set of theses by responding to the challenges put to him by the audience. The theses usually came from the lectures of the professor who presided over the defense. It was the live event that counted, not the written word. The written word needed to be published in advance so that presiding professor, responding student, and questioning audience could work from the same printed page. But it was ancillary to the intellectual event. It functioned, in the fashion of a degree recital, like the score for an intellectual performance. The test turned on the student's performance, not on the contents of the score.

Who wrote the dissertation was therefore a secondary question. Most commonly it was the professor. Often, a whole series of theses defended by a series of students would later on be published in a single volume under the professor's name as a coherent book devoted to a particular subject. A good example is Conring's own work on the circulation of the blood.[7] Sometimes the professor worked

---

[6] Readers interested in more information and a detailed examination of the evidence supporting the points made in the following paragraphs are referred to Constantin Fasolt, "Author and Authenticity in Conring's *New Discourse on the Roman-German Emperor*: A Seventeenth-Century Case Study," *Renaissance Quarterly* 54 (2001): 188–220.

[7] *De sanguinis generatione et motu naturali opus novum* (Helmstedt: H. Müller, 1643), which consists of ten separate dissertations that had been published under Conring's supervision.

together with the student. But only rarely was the student sole author of the text, and when he was, there was good reason to make that clear. This is what Conring did with a dissertation that he himself defended while he was still a student in Leiden. Precisely because it was unusual that he, as student, claimed sole authorship for the dissertation, he made sure to say so on the title page.[8] Other things being equal, seventeenth-century dissertations are therefore justifiably attributed to the professor presiding at the defense.

Such is the case with the dissertation that Bogislaus Otho von Hoym defended under Conring's presidency in 1641. Von Hoym was no distinguished thinker. We know nothing of his later career, we have no books he published, and we have no reason to believe that he did more than put Conring's lectures into writing. As he explained on the title page, his dissertation was mostly (*praecipue*) based on Conring's lectures.[9] Whatever he added—assuming he added anything—probably consisted of references to primary and secondary literature and condensations, elaborations, or reformulations of points made by Conring himself. As far as intellectual substance was concerned, it scarcely reflected von Hoym's ideas.

Conring had been lecturing on the Holy Roman Empire since the mid-1630s. He had already begun to express some of his views on the relationship between Germany and the Roman empire in prefaces to his editions of Tacitus's *Germania* and Aristotle's *Politics*.[10] By 1641 his views were well developed. The longer, more detailed, and more accomplished *Book on the Roman Empire of the Germans* that Conring published soon after, in 1644, makes almost precisely the same case as the dissertation of 1641, and sometimes does so verbatim.[11] Conring republished von Hoym's dissertation in 1674, and when he did so, he made only

---

[8] *Theses variae de morali prudentia* (Leiden: Patius, 1629; repr. in *Opera*, 6:335–37). At the end of the title page Conring identifies himself as "A. & R.", that is, author and respondent.

[9] The full title is *Exercitatio de imperatore Romano Germanico quam ex discursibus praecipue viri clarissimi, excellentissimi atque experientissimi Hermanni Conringii philosoph.[iae] ac med.[icinae] d.[octoris] huiusque in illustri Iulia Academia professoris celeberrimi, fautoris ac praeceptoris plurimum honorandi desumtam eodem praeside examini publico submittit Bogislaus Otho ab Hoym eq.[ues] Pomeranus. Ad diem IIX Maii. In Novo Iuleo Maiori.*

[10] "Praefatio de historiarum, Germanorum inprimis, studiis," in Tacitus, *De moribus Germanorum*, ed. Hermann Conring (Helmstedt: Lucius, 1635; repr. in *Opera*, 5:253–78); "Praefatio in politicam Aristotelis," in Aristotle, *Politicorum libri octo*, trans. Obertus Giphanius, ed. Hermann Conring (Helmstedt: Lucius, 1637; repr. in *Opera*, 1:117–28).

[11] *De Germanorum imperio Romano liber unus* (Helmstedt: H. Müller and M. Richter, 1644; repr. in *Opera*, 1:26–107).

one significant change that served to modify the dissertation's radical conclusion, but did not really change the substance of the argument.[12] Most revealingly, in the lectures on the Holy Roman Empire that he gave later in his life and that remained unpublished until Johann Wilhelm Goebel included them in his edition of Conring's *Opera*, Conring did not hesitate to call von Hoym's piece "my dissertation on the German empire" and to recommend it as a reliable condensation of the very *Book on the Roman Empire of the Germans* that he had ostensibly written in order to correct the damage done to his reputation by the unauthorized publication of von Hoym's dissertation as a *New Discourse on the Roman-German Emperor*.[13]

In short, the dissertation reproduced in the *New Discourse* is anything but the work of Bogislaus Otho von Hoym. It is rather an especially interesting source of information about Conring's ideas. It presents these ideas in an unguarded early version, before Conring had had the chance to polish their sharpest edges. That is why he was infuriated by the pirated edition.[14] It was not that he disagreed with the ideas. They were his own. It was that the ideas had escaped from his control before he had been able to dress them properly for their appearance in the public sphere. That makes the *New Discourse* particularly worth reading. And that is why I have chosen to translate it here.

Scholarly examination of Conring's work has not yet reached a point at which it would be possible to locate him with any great precision on the landscape of early modern intellectual history. But some general observations will help to orient the reader. Conring stands in the middle of a continuous history leading almost directly from Luther and Melanchthon to Leibniz and Lessing, from the Protestant Reformation to the German Enlightenment. His father and both of his grandfathers were Lutheran ministers. He himself studied at a university profoundly shaped by the influence of Melanchthon. His teachers had been taught by Johannes Caselius (1533–1613), and Caselius had been taught by Melanchthon. His students included Johann Christian von Boineburg. Boineburg

---

[12] "De imperatore Romano Germanico," in Hermann Conring, *Exercitationes academicae de republica imperii Germanici* (Helmstedt: J. Müller, 1674), 32–72.

[13] "Caeterum tempore Ottonis M.[agni] qui praeterpropter 100. annis vixit post Carolum M.[agnum] ipsius felicitate regnum Germaniae, quod tum regnum Francorum dictum, alterno [sic] foedere iungebatur regno Italiae et imperio Romano, quod ostensum a me in libro de imperio Romano Germanico. Quibus liber iste non est in manibus, legant disputationem meam de imperio Germanico, quae quasi est compendium eius rei": "Discursus ad Lampadium posterior ex manuscripto," in *Opera*, 2:239.

[14] For his criticism of the *New Discourse* see the prefatory matter to *De Germanorum imperio Romano liber unus* (Helmstedt: H. Müller and M. Richter, 1644), in *Opera*, 1:26–27.

was the man who discovered Leibniz and helped him to rise to intellectual prominence. Leibniz would go on to serve the same family of dukes whom Conring served as well. He became director of the Herzog August Bibliothek that nowadays hosts scholars from all over the globe. And Lessing succeeded Leibniz in that capacity. *Nathan the Wise* was written across the street from the great library Duke August had with Conring's help created in the middle decades of the seventeenth century. Conring, one is tempted to say, is the middle link in a chain of personal affiliations connecting Luther to Lessing. He was a Lutheran, no doubt. But he had experienced greater religious freedom in the Netherlands than could be had in Germany during the Thirty Years War. He was determined to extend that freedom to Germany and to liberate politics from religion.

In terms of his scholarly and scientific leanings, Conring is perhaps best characterized as a modernizing Aristotelian. He was deeply impressed by the systematic intellectual coherence of Aristotle's philosophy and he never left the intellectual foundations with which Aristotle furnished him. He was no follower of the mechanical philosophy of Descartes, nor did he much like Hobbes's new science. Mathematics played no great role in his life. He was a humanist. He worked with language and with words. But he was thoroughly informed about recent advances in scholarship and science. His impassioned defense of Harvey's theory of blood circulation puts him in the forefront of the medicine of his day. He focused much favorable attention on Machiavelli in order to alert his contemporaries to the autonomy of politics from morality, law, and religion. From Jean Bodin he adopted ideas of sovereignty and state, and from Hugo Grotius he acquired an interest in theories of natural and international law that put him at odds with Aristotelianism. His life's work was designed to respond to the challenge with which the emancipation of politics from law and religion confronted early modern Europeans. He did not develop the response as far as Locke or Pufendorf would. Locke and Pufendorf, both born in 1632, belonged to the next generation. But he was moving in the same direction. It was Conring and Conring's generation—the generation whose intellectual maturity coincides with the Peace of Westphalia—who first managed to secure the field of social and political thought for cultivation with ideas of natural law and individual rights that still shape political debate today.

Chronology[15]

Events in Conring's Life

1606	On 9 November Hermann Conring is born in Norden, East Frisia, as the ninth of ten children
1611	Survives the plague; six sisters die
1612	German school in Norden
1613-20	Latin school in Norden; reads Lipsius, Scaliger, and Heinsius
1620–25	Studies philosophy at University of Helmstedt; taught by Martini, Diephold, Heidmann, Gran, Calixt
1623	Forced by the war to return to Norden
1624	Resumes studies in Helmstedt
1625	Forced by war to return to Norden for second time

Other Events

Birth of Rembrandt (d. 1669) and Corneille (d. 1684)	1606
Birth of Milton (d. 1674)	1608
King Henry IV assassinated	1610
King Louis XIII	1610–43
King Gustavus Adolphus	1611–32
Death of Cervantes (b. 1547) and Shakespeare (b. 1564)	1616
Thirty Years War	1618–48
Emperor Ferdinand II	1619–37
The Mayflower lands	1620
War between Spain and the Dutch Provinces	1621–48
Birth of Pascal (d. 1662)	1623
Cardinal Richelieu chief minister of France	1624–42
Grotius, *The Law of War and Peace*	1625
King Charles I	1625–49

---

[15] I have based this chronology on the "Zeittafel" in Patricia Herberger and Michael Stolleis, *Hermann Conring, 1606–1681: Ein Gelehrter der Universität Helmstedt* (Wolfenbüttel: Herzog August Bibliothek, 1981), 8–9. I have added the titles (in English) of some of Conring's most important publications and information about parallel events that may help to situate Conring in the context of German and European intellectual and political history.

1626-31	Studies medicine at University of Leiden; taught by Vossius, Heinsius, Barlaeus, and Burgersdicius	Death of Bacon (b. 1561)	1626
		Dutch purchase Manhattan	
1627	*Disputation on the Physics of Innate Heat*	Birth of Bossuet (d. 1704)	1627
		Petition of Right	1628
		William Harvey, *Circulation of the Blood*	
1629	*Various Theses on Morals*	Edict of Restitution	1629
1630	*Disputation on the Origin of Forms*	Death of Kepler (b. 1571)	1630
		Sweden enters Thirty Years War	1630–48
1631	Leaves Leiden and returns to Germany; tutor to the son of Chancellor Arnold Engelbrecht in Brunswick; befriends Jacob Lampadius and turns to history	Death of John Donne (b. 1572)	1631
		Birth of John Dryden (d. 1700)	
1632-37	Professor of natural philosophy at University of Helmstedt; experiments on blood circulation	Queen Christina of Sweden	1632–54
		Birth of Spinoza (d. 1677), Pufendorf (d. 1694), and Locke (d. 1704)	1632
1632	*In Praise of Aristotle* (inaugural lecture)	Galileo, *Dialogue on the Two Chief World Systems*	
1634	*Medical Disputation on Scurvey* earns Conring licentiate in medicine; edits Lampadius, *Treatise on the Roman-German Commonwealth*; begins to offer private courses on history and politics	Imperial victory at Nördlingen	1634
		Death of Wallenstein (b. 1583)	
		Richelieu establishes the Académie Française	
1635	Edits Tacitus, *Germania*	Peace of Prague	1635
		France enters Thirty Years War	1635–48
		Duke August the Younger of Brunswick-Wolfenbüttel	1635–66

1636	On 21 April Conring obtains doctorates in medicine and philosophy; marries Anna Maria Stucke (b. 1616) the same day	Charter for Harvard College	1636
1637-81	Professor of medicine at University of Helmstedt	Emperor Ferdinand III	1637-57
1637	Edits Aristotle, *Politics*	Descartes, *Discourse on Method*	1637
1638	*Introduction to Natural Philosophy*	Galileo, *Discorsi*	1638
1639	*Civil Prudence: Its Nature and Its Treatment by the Best Authorities*	Death of Campanella (b. 1568)	1639
		Birth of Racine (d. 1699)	
		Frederick William I of Prussia	1640-88
1641	*Exercise on the Roman German Emperor*, respondent B. O. von Hoym	Descartes, *Meditations*	1641
1642	*New Discourse on the Roman-German Emperor*	Death of Galileo (b. 1564)	1642
		English Civil War	1642-48
1643	*The Generation and Circulation of the Blood by Nature*	Birth of Newton (d. 1727)	1643
		King Louis XIV	1643-1715
	Historical Commentary on the Origin of German Law	Cardinal Mazarin chief minister of France	1643-61
1644	*The Roman Empire of the Germans*	Poyarkov reaches the estuary of the Amur	1644
1645	*The Condition of the German Body in Antiquity and the Present*	Death of Grotius (b. 1583)	1645
		Birth of Leibniz (d. 1716)	1646
1647	*Innate Heat or Animal Fire*	Birth of Pierre Bayle (d. 1706)	1647
1648	*The Hermetic Medicine of the Ancient Egyptians and the New Medicine of the Paracelsians*	Peace of Westphalia ends Thirty Years War	1648

1648	Irenaeus Eubulus (pseudonym), *A Catholic Deliberation in Favor of Lasting Peace with Protestants*	Peace of the Hague ends Spanish-Dutch War	1648
		Royal Academy founded in Paris	
1649	Appointed court physician and privy councilor to Juliane of East Frisia	Execution of Charles I	1649
		Death of Lampadius (b. 1593)	
		English Commonwealth under Cromwell	1649–53
1650	Visits Stockholm at invitation of Queen Christina; appointed Swedish court physician and royal councilor	Death of Descartes (b. 1596)	1650
		Hobbes, *The Elements of Law*	
1650-81	Holds a second chair as professor of politics at University of Helmstedt	Otto von Guericke invents the air pump	
1651	*Dissertation on Reason of State*	Hobbes, *Leviathan*	1651
1653	Inherits an estate and large house in Helmstedt from his father-in-law	Mazarin defeats the Fronde	1653
		Oliver Cromwell, Lord Protector	1653–58
1654	*The Borders of the German Empire*	Death of Oxenstierna (b. 1583)	1654
	Introduction to the Whole Art of Medicine	Queen Christina resigns	
		Birth of Bernoulli (d. 1705)	
1655	*The Rights of Mainz in Crowning the King of the Romans*	Spain loses Jamaica to England	1655
	Cyriacus Thrasymachus (pseudonym), *The Justice of Sweden's War Against Poland*	Death of Heinsius (b. 1580)	
		War between Sweden and Poland	1655–60
1656	New edition of Aristotle, *Politics*	Death of Calixt (b. 1586)	1656

1657	*On Lasting Peace Between Estates of the German Empire That Are Divided by Religion*	Death of Harvey (b. 1578)	1657
1658	Appointed court physician and councilor to King Charles X of Sweden	Death of Cromwell (b. 1599)	1658
		Birth of Purcell (d. 1695)	
	Defense of the Palatinate's Imperial Vicariate	Emperor Leopold I	1658–1705
		Peace of the Pyrenees between Spain and France	1659
1660	Appointed privy councilor to Duke August of Brunswick-Wolfenbüttel	Peace of Oliva between Sweden and Poland	1660
		Death of Velázquez (b. 1599)	
	Edits Machiavelli's *Prince* and begins regular lectures on the states of Europe	Stuart Restoration	1660–88
1661	*Political Commentary on Machiavelli's Book on the Prince*	King Louis XIV rules in person	1661–1715
1662	*Civil Prudence*	Royal Society founded in London	1662
1663	Draws pension from Louis XIV	Permanent Diet at Regensburg	1663
	Propolitica or Brief Introduction to Political Philosophy	New Amsterdam becomes New York	1664
1665	Edits Scipio Chiaramonti, *How to Infer a Person's Character*	Plague in London	1665
		La Rochefoucauld, *Réflexions*	
1666	*Collected Prefatory Letters*	Great Fire in London	1666
	On Trade and Commerce	Death of Duke August of Brunswick-Wolfenbüttel (b. 1579)	
1669	Resigns Swedish positions; becomes Danish councilor of state instead	Death of Rembrandt (b. 1606)	1669
		Grimmelshausen, *Simplicius Simplicissimus*	
	Two Books on Hermetic Medicine		

1671	New edition of Lampadius, *The Roman-German Commonwealth*	Milton, *Paradise Regained* and *Samson Agonistes*	1671
1672	*The Authenticity of Emperor Louis's Charter for the Convent of Lindau*	Pufendorf, *The Law of Nature and Nations*	1672
		War between France and the Netherlands	1672–88
1673	French pension ends	Death of Molière (b. 1622)	1673
1674	*Academic Exercises on the German Empire*	Death of Milton (b. 1608)	1674
1675	*A Treasury of Commonwealths*, pirated publication of lectures on states of Europe by Philip Oldenburger	Death of Vermeer (b. 1632)	1675
		Nat Bacon's Rebellion	1676
		Death of Hobbes (b. 1588)	1679
1680	Retires from teaching	Death of La Rochefoucauld (b. 1613)	1680
1681	*The Borders of the German Empire, Book Three*	French annexation of Strasbourg	1681
	On 12 December Hermann Conring dies in Helmstedt		
1694	Conring's widow dies; library is auctioned off by son	Death of Pufendorf (b. 1632)	1694
		Birth of Voltaire (d. 1778)	
		Birth of Lessing (d. 1781) and Edmund Burke (d. 1797)	1729
1730	Conring's *Opera* published in Brunswick by Johann Wilhelm Goebel		

Notes on the English Translation

The purpose of this translation is simply to make the text of the *New Discourse on the Roman-German Emperor* available to readers of English.[16] I have not tried to reproduce Conring's grammar and phrasing exactly as they appear in the Latin. I have rather tried to capture the flow of his argument without doing violence to his terminology or abolishing all traces of his style of thought—a style very much in keeping with the temperament of his times. I have often changed the sequence of clauses, turned the passive into the active voice, changed relative clauses into complete sentences, replaced pronouns with the nouns to which they refer, and added words that can be left implied in Latin but need to be made explicit in English. On the whole I have simplified the text as much as seemed desirable in order to get Conring's point across while staying as close to the Latin as necessary.

The subject of the *New Discourse on the Roman-German Emperor* is Conring's reconstruction of the history of the Roman empire and its relationship to Germany from antiquity to the early modern period. I have made no systematic attempt to compare Conring's own views on that subject with those taken by experts in history today.[17] But the reader should at least be warned not to confuse the two. All the signals are that Conring played a pivotal role in German historiography. But that means neither that his understanding of the history of the Roman empire overall can be trusted nor that it has not long since been proved to be misleading, unfounded, or plain wrong on this or that particular issue. Sometimes the particular issue concerns major turning-points. Such, for example, is the case with his interpretation of the relationship between Otto the Great and the papacy. On that score his critical abilities seem to have failed him so conveniently that Arno Seifert has characterized his account as the creation of an "Ottonian legend" that owed more to wishful thinking than to historical truth.[18]

---

[16] For a brief analysis of the argument see Constantin Fasolt, "A Question of Right: Hermann Conring's *New Discourse on the Roman-German Emperor*," *Sixteenth Century Journal* 28 (1997): 739–58. For Conring's theory of history more generally speaking see idem, "Conring on History," in *Supplementum Festivum: Studies in Honor of Paul Oskar Kristeller*, ed. James Hankins, John Monfasani, and Frederick Purnell, MRTS 49 (Binghamton: Medieval and Renaissance Texts and Studies, 1987), 563–87.

[17] For more information about the relevant scholarship, see the guide to further reading below, p. 87.

[18] Arno Seifert, "Conring und die 'Ottonische Legende'," in *Der Rückzug der biblischen Prophetie von der neueren Geschichte* (Cologne: Böhlau, 1990), 165–86. Cf. Walter Ullmann, "The Origins of the *Ottonianum*," *Cambridge Historical Journal* 11 (1952): 114–28.

A few issues deserve special mention. One of them is Conring's habit of paying respect to fine conceptual distinctions by pairing terms with slightly different meanings. "Right and legitimate," "acquisitions and possessions," "titles and rights," "names and titles," and "possess and retain" are good examples. In the precisely articulated grammatical structures that Latin makes possible, those pairings do not clutter the text. In English they do. Unless they play an appreciable role in the context of Conring's argument, I have therefore collapsed them into a single term. That procedure has a cost: it conceals information about the finer points of Conring's argument. But seeing that readers genuinely interested in the finer points of Conring's argument will in any case be obliged to consult the Latin original (for which even the most literal translation can only be an approximation), and seeing that the Latin is close at hand, the cost seems minimal.

Something similar may be said about Conring's use of technical terms. On the whole I have tried to use the same English word for a given technical term in Latin—"federated" in the place of *foederati*, for example, and "ownership" in the place of *dominium*. But I have also felt free to use different English words for the same Latin words if the Latin seemed to put no particular emphasis on the technical meaning, or if the context seemed to require it for another reason. I have thus sometimes used "allied" instead of "federated" for *foederati*, and "lordship" or "dominion" instead of "ownership" for *dominium*. This variability applies especially to the word *Caesar*, which I have translated as "Caesar" when it appears in the title of a given emperor or when it is contrasted with *imperator*, but as "emperor" in almost all other cases.

One word requires more detailed commentary: *respublica*, the "public thing" or "thing of the people." *Respublica* (usually spelled by Conring as one word) is an important, perhaps the single most important, term in Conring's political vocabulary. It is also notoriously difficult to translate. It has several different meanings for which there are no good modern English equivalents. These meanings had been undergoing significant changes for some time before Conring was writing and they conflicted with one another. Jean Bodin, for example, saw nothing wrong with using *respublica*, or its French equivalent *république*, to refer to absolute monarchy. Though his most famous work was one of the most significant endorsements of absolute monarchy to have been written in early modern times, he chose to call it *Six Books of the Republic*, not *Six Books of Sovereignty*, or *Six Books of the State*, much less *Six Books of Absolute Monarchy*. On the other hand, *respublica* is regularly taken to refer to a "republican" form of government that was just about as directly opposed to absolute monarchy as can be imagined.

Translators usually try to steer clear of trouble by translating *respublica* as "commonwealth." There are good reasons for that choice. "Commonwealth" does not translate *respublica* exactly. It refers to what is "common" rather than "public"—not necessarily an insignificant distinction—and it is used to designate a body politic as a whole, not so much its constitution, much less a particular form of constitution, as *respublica* can do. But at least "commonwealth" is capable of referring to any kind of independent state (at least so long as it is not a full-blown tyranny, which does perhaps not deserve to be called a state at all), including not only states with a "republican" constitution, but also states ruled by absolute monarchs. "Commonwealth" is thus blessed with a certain capacity for duplicating the confusion between any kind of state and a particular kind of state that is so commonly associated with the term *respublica*. Perhaps that was what persuaded Richard Knolles to prefer "commonwealth" over "republic" in his translation of Jean Bodin's *Six livres de la république* as *Six Bookes of a Commonweale* in 1606.[19]

Fortunately Hermann Conring valued precision. Well aware that *respublica* had more than one meaning, he made every effort to define those meanings as clearly as he could. There are many places in his writings where he considered the question in passing. He also supervised no less than four dissertations that were explicitly devoted to the question.[20] And late in his life he reviewed the different meanings of *respublica* concisely and lucidly in his commentary on Lampadius's *De republica Romano-Germanica* of 1671.[21] Since Conring had worked on this commentary for many years, we may presume that it represents his considered point of view.

According to Conring's commentary on Lampadius's *De republica Romano-Germanica*, *respublica* has four basic meanings. First and most commonly, *respublica* means "the whole body of a civil society—what the Romans once called a *civitas*, even though nowadays the term *civitas* is mainly used to refer to a city

---

[19] Jean Bodin, *The Six Bookes of a Commonweale. Written by I. Bodin . . . Out of the French and Latine Copies Done into English by Richard Knolles* (London: G. Bishop, 1606).

[20] These are, in chronological order, the *Disputatio politica de rebuspublicis in genere*, respondent G. Poch (Helmstedt: Lucius, 1639; repr. in *Opera*, 3:816–22); *Disputatio politica de rebuspublicis in genere*, respondent E. Nissen (Helmstedt: H. Müller, 1651; this dissertation was not reprinted in Conring's *Opera*, perhaps because the title misled Goebel into thinking that it was identical with the dissertation defended by Poch in 1639); *De politia sive republica in specie sic dicta*, respondent J. E. Busch (Helmstedt: H. Müller, 1652; repr. in *Opera*, 3:774–78); and *Disputatio politica de republica in communi*, respondent O. J. von Osten gen. Sacken (Helmstedt: H. Müller, 1653; repr. in *Opera*, 3:763–74). Also worth mentioning are the *Exercitatio politica de optima republica*, respondent J. Behrens (Helmstedt: H. Müller, 1652; repr. in *Opera*, 3:823–39), and especially Hermann Conring's own *Exercitatio historico-politica de notitia singularis alicuius reipublicae*, printed posthumously by Goebel in *Opera*, 4:1–43.

[21] See note (a) in his edition of Lampadius's *De republica Romano-Germanica* (Helmstedt: H. Müller, 1671), in *Opera*, 2:22–25.

or a town [rather than to an independent body politic]."[22] *Respublica* in this first acceptation is used to distinguish one especially important kind of association from all others, namely, the kind of association that enjoys independence and sovereignty from those that do not, such as associations of husbands and wives, parents and children, masters and slaves, and villages, as Aristotle had famously explained.[23] In this sense, *respublica* refers to a body politic or "civil society" as a whole, without attention to the constitution by which one body politic may be distinguished from another. It presupposes the sovereignty of the body politic to which it refers. It thus means what we would nowadays most naturally call a state, and on occasion a polity or a commonwealth.

Second, *respublica* refers to a certain part or aspect of the body politic, namely, "the public regime of any kind of polity."[24] Here *respublica* is used to distinguish, not states from other kinds of association, but one part of a state from another part of the same state, such as its government from its citizens, its form from its matter, or its public from its private side. In this sense, *respublica* means "the organization or constitution of civil society, either in terms of [the relationship between] its various powers, or most particularly in terms of that one power that is supreme above all others."[25] It thus refers to the constitution of a state as embodied in the offices with responsibility for its public functions, and especially the supreme office of the sovereign ruler.

Third, *respublica* can be used *par excellence* to refer to "that organization of a body politic which is the best among those in which the people rule, namely, the one in which the body politic is actually governed by the people as a whole, and not merely by that part of the people which is poor, but claims to represent the people as a whole because it is more numerous than the rest."[26] Here *respublica*

---

[22] "Reipublicae vox variae est significationis. Capitur enim hodie perfrequenter pro integro aliquo civilis societatis corpore, quod Latini olim civitatem dixerunt, etsi nunc vocabulum illud plerumque urbem notet": *Opera*, 2:22. I have translated *civilis societas* as "civil society" knowing full well that this also requires a lot of commentary—but not here.

[23] Aristotle, *Politics* 1.1–2, 1252a1–1253a40.

[24] "Significat deinde regimen publicum civitatis cuiuslibet": *Opera*, 2:22.

[25] "Ordo sive constitutio civilis societatis, cum ratione ceterarum potestatum, tum praecipue ratione eius, quae omnium est summa vel domina": *Opera*, 2:22. This, Conring pointed out, was the definition that Aristotle had offered in bk. 3, chap. 4 of his *Politics* (as numbered in the edition Conring used; in modern editions, this is bk. 3, chap. 6).

[26] "Iam olim porro κατ' ἐξοχὴν respublica, ut et Graece πολιτεία, audiit ordo ille civitatis, qui inter populares est optimus atque revera ab universo populo regitur, non autem ab ea dumtaxat populi parte, quae tenuioris est fortunae, cum praestet autem multitudine, solet populi nomen sibi vendicare": *Opera*, 2:22. For this sense Conring referred to Aristotle's *Politics*, bk. 4 chap. 9, where Aristotle described the "polity" as a mean between oligarchy and democracy.

is used to distinguish a "republican" constitution from constitutions such as aristocracy, oligarchy, democracy, or monarchy. It refers to the particular form of constitution in which power is genuinely in the hands of the people as a whole, and not merely in the hands of a part of the people, however small or numerous that part may be. In this sense, *respublica* is what Aristotle called a "polity," what Conring called a "*respublica* par excellence," and what we still have in mind when we speak of "republics."

Fourth, and finally, *respublica* "is nowadays used for any kind of government that is not monarchical, like aristocratic, oligarchic, democratic, and [of course] republican government par excellence, as well as every kind of government that is composed of these."[27] In this sense, *respublica* is used to refer to any kind of constitution just so long as it is not monarchy. It includes a whole variety of constitutions, like aristocracy, oligarchy, and democracy, for no other reason than that they are united by a common opposition to monarchy. One may assume that this meaning reflects the growing importance of "absolutism" in Conring's time, because it lumps all other forms of government together, just so long as they are not monarchical. We may perhaps translate this meaning of *respublica* as "a constitutional regime," as opposed to absolute monarchy.

These four definitions of *respublica* have a logical relationship to one another. They proceed from the broader and more general to the narrower and more particular. The first refers to any kind of sovereign state; the second, to the constitution of any kind of sovereign state; the third, to a particular ("republican") constitution; and the fourth, to all constitutions opposed to a particular ("monarchical") constitution. The first refers to *respublica* as a whole or genus; the other three refer to parts or species of the whole. The second refers to a part of the whole without distinguishing between different varieties; the third and fourth both refer to different varieties of that part, but the third refers positively to the variety of constitution that serves the good of the people as a whole, while the fourth refers negatively to any variety of constitution that is not monarchical.

The four meanings of *respublica* that Conring distinguished in his commentary on Lampadius in 1671 parallel four meanings that he had already distinguished in the *Disputatio politica de rebuspublicis in genere* published more than thirty years earlier in 1639, and defended by his student G. Poch, the oldest piece of writing in which Conring dealt systematically with the various meanings of *respublica* of which I am aware. The four definitions given there are not quite identical to those in the commentary on Lampadius, nor are they listed in the

---

[27] "Denique respublica dici solet hodie regimen omne civitatis quod non est μοναρχικὸν, ut comprehendat et aristocratiam, et oligarchiam, et democratiam, et rempublicam κατ' ἐξοχὴν dictam, omnesque ex iis compositas species": *Opera*, 2:22.

same order.[28] In 1671, the definition of *respublica* in the sense of "any independent state" came first. In 1639 it came last, as something of an afterthought to the three main definitions that preceded it. It came last because it referred to a meaning that was distinguished by "rather frequent usage," but not authenticated by inclusion in Aristotle's *Politics*. In 1639 there was also no clear mention of *respublica* in the sense of "constitutional government," as opposed to monarchy. Instead it was defined as "that form of government in which sovereignty is in the hands of the people." These differences illustrate the decreasing importance of Aristotle's *Politics* in Conring's thought and the growing importance of two other factors: the "state" and the sharpening distinction between absolute monarchy and constitutional government. But they are still variations within the terms of a single conceptual framework. One may conclude that Conring developed the views set forth in the commentary on Lampadius early in life, refined them over many years of reading and research, and reasserted them in 1671 with clarity and confidence. They certainly informed his usage of the term in the *New Discourse*.

There are a few occasions in the *New Discourse* on which one of the narrower meanings of *respublica* may have been on Conring's mind. In chapter forty, for example, he writes that the pope usurped lordship over all *regna* and *respublicas* of the world. There *regna* is contrasted with *respublicas*. I have therefore translated that phrase as "kingdoms and republics." But in the very same chapter forty Conring also says that there are as many *respublicae* as there are *summae potestates*. *Summa potestas* is the term Conring uses more or less consistently for "sovereignty." In that place *respublica* is thus explicitly defined by the presence of sovereignty, as in the first and most basic of the four senses he distinguished in his commentary on Lampadius: where there is a sovereign, there is a *respublica*, regardless of whether or not the *respublica* in question is a monarchy, an aristocracy, a democracy, or a mixture of these. That is the meaning that prevails throughout the *New Discourse*. It may even have been the meaning Conring had in mind on that single occasion in chapter forty where he opposed *regna* to *respublicae*. When he thought of *regna*, he may well not have been thinking of sovereign "kingdoms," but of

---

[28] "Dicamus tamen aliquid, et quidem de varia huius vocis [reipublicae] acceptione, quae potissimum triplex apud Aristotelem invenitur. Scilicet universe primo sumatur pro qualibet ordinatione magistratus summi, quando nempe dicitur respublicas esse vel mixtas vel simplices, item vel unius vel paucorum, aut etiam plurium. Arctiore acceptione venit, quando mixtionem oligarchiae et democratiae interpretamur. Arctissime autem, cum indigitatur illa forma in qua penes populum suprema dignitas est seu maiestas. Addi porro potest et quarta acceptio satis usitata, qua respublica est ipsa civitas, suis administrandi legibus instructa": *Disputatio politica de rebuspublicis in genere* (Helmstedt: Lucius, 1639), quoted from *Opera*, 3:818.

"realms" comprising an agglomeration of sovereigns under some kind of imperial hegemon, or perhaps lacking sovereignty altogether.

That makes the choice easy: with two exceptions—the example just given and the "republic of Ragusa" mentioned in chapter fifty-six—I have translated *respublica* as "state." "State" seems more appropriate than "commonwealth" because of the emphasis that Conring's definition of *respublica* (in the first sense) placed on the presence of a sovereign power. From his perspective, like Bodin's, it was sovereignty that made it possible to speak of a *respublica* in the first place. Without sovereignty, there was no *respublica*. Whether or not the *respublica* was a commonwealth in the narrower "republican" or "constitutional" senses of the term was a secondary question.

My translation of the *New Discourse* is based on a close comparison of the *Discursus novus de imperatore Romano-Germanico* of 1642 with two other versions of the same text: the original *Exercitatio de imperatore Romano Germanico* published in Helmstedt in 1641 and defended by Bogislaus Otho von Hoym under Conring's personal supervision; and the revised version of the *Exercitatio* that Conring included in his *Exercitationes academicae de republica imperii Germanici* in 1674. The differences among these three versions are relatively few. For the most part they are limited to matters of orthography, the order of words, and misprints corrected or newly introduced in the later versions. Where such differences have no bearing on the meaning of the text I have omitted them. Where they do, I have pointed them out in the footnotes.[29]

In order to keep the relationship among the different versions of the text as clear as possible I have translated the *Discursus novus de imperatore Romano-Germanico* of 1642 in the main body of the text, including its errors. I have relegated everything else to the footnotes. In the footnotes I have also pointed out a few misprints and errors that are shared by the *New Discourse* with all other versions of the *Exercitatio de imperatore Romano Germanico* because they illustrate the close relationship among the different versions.

Readers should know that there are two other versions of the text that I have excluded from consideration. One is the version Johann Wilhelm Goebel printed in his edition of Conring's *Opera*, 1:528–42. This is is an entirely derivative reprint of the revised version Conring himself published in 1674. I have also ignored the footnotes that Goebel added because they reflect Goebel's work rather than Conring's. The other version was published under the title "De imperatore Romano Germanico discursus historico-politicus" on pages 275–309 of *De imperii Germanici republica acroamata sex historico-politica* (Embrun: Apud Societatem, 1655),

---

[29] For further details on the differences among these editions and their relationship to one another see Fasolt, "Author and Authenticity."

a pirated collection of several of Conring's writings on the empire. This was not just another unauthorized reprint published without Conring's permission, as the *New Discourse* had been. It was rather an entirely unreliable hybrid that combined selected passages from the *New Discourse* with other passages taken from Conring's *De Germanorum imperio Romano* of 1644. It furnishes excellent evidence for the interest with which Conring's ideas were received, and it testifies shamelessly to the freedom with which its publishers saw fit to reconfigure Conring's writings. But it changes the text of the *New Discourse* beyond recognition. I have therefore not used it here.

Conring's way of identifying his sources deserves some explanation. When he refers to a passage in another book, he usually mentions the author or editor, the title, and the relevant chapter or whatever other type of subdivision is appropriate. He never mentions publishers or places and dates of publication, and only rarely page numbers. That is a useful practice because it frees the reader from having to use exactly the same edition that Conring used. I have therefore left it unchanged, except for a few cases where chapters are so long as to make checking time-consuming, or where confusion is likely for some other reason. I have, however, expanded Conring's abbreviations and used the footnotes to give more detailed bibliographical information about the writings to which he referred. For the convenience of readers who would like to get a quick overview of the nature and range of Conring's reading, I have compiled all of the sources Conring cited in the *New Discourse* in a list of "Works Cited in the *New Discourse*."[30]

I have verified all of Conring's references, but I have made no systematic attempt to identify the particular editions on which he relied. In many cases I simply used the early modern edition that happened to be at my disposal. Sometimes that must have been the edition on which Conring relied as well because it is the only edition that was ever published. If I was able to use more than one early modern edition, I used whichever seemed most likely to be available to other readers. Where there is a recent or critical edition, I have usually preferred it over early modern editions. In cases where there are noteworthy differences between early modern and more recent editions, I mentioned both. Where I knew of translations into English, I added references to that effect. In all cases I listed only editions that I was able to consult myself.

Some of the books cited by Conring appear in Migne's *Patrologia Latina*, a convenient and widely available collection of Latin texts written before 1198.[31]

---

[30] See below, pp. 97–104.

[31] Jacques-Paul Migne, *Patrologiae cursus completus, series Latina*, 221 vols. (Paris: Migne, 1844–1902).

Wherever that is the case, I have added a reference to that effect, using the abbreviation *PL* followed by volume and page or column numbers.

The *New Discourse* is divided into fifty-six theses or chapters consecutively numbered with capital Roman numerals. They have no titles that would help the reader to recognize the logical structure of the argument. I have therefore divided the text into sections and subsections and given headings to each section in order to make the structure of the argument more transparent and identify the topics with which Conring deals at any given point. Readers may well disagree with me about the decisions I have made in dividing the text into sections and assigning headings to them. Still I hope that they will help to understand how Conring defined his subject, what he considered to be the most important questions, and how he went about answering them. In order to avoid any confusion with Conring's own text, headings I added are enclosed in brackets and numbered with capital letters, lower-case letters and, where necessary, lower-case Roman numerals, e.g., C.b.ii.

Notes on the Latin Text

The purpose of these notes is to clarify some characteristics of Conring's Latin and to identify the changes I have made to it for the purposes of this edition. The changes are minor. They are limited to matters of punctuation, spelling, capitalization, abbreviations, and the use of italics.

Concerning punctuation, I have avoided the temptation to discern uniform rules behind Conring's practice—a difficult if not impossible task—much less to implement them with mechanical regularity. I have rather tried to listen closely to the rhythm of his Latin and to reconcile it with the needs of contemporary readers. I have accordingly felt free to remove commas that seemed to clutter the text, and insert them where that helped to clarify syntactical relationships. I have also replaced most colons and semi-colons with commas or full stops, depending on the context. But I used colons more regularly than Conring in order to introduce direct quotations.

Concerning spelling, I consistently replaced j with i (*ius* not *jus*), u with v (*evangelista* not *euangelista*), and qu with c (*cur* not *quur*; *cum* not *quum*; *consecutus* not *consequuutus*). I removed the diacritical signs Conring often placed on accented vowels (ò, è, à, â), expanded contractions (æ, œ, and e-cedille), and regularized the usage of e, oe, and ae (*saeculum* not *seculum*; *caelum* not *coelum*; *paene* not *poene*; but *pleraque* not *plaeraque*; *heredes* not *haeredes*; *ceterum* not *caeterum*). I also removed elisions and assimilations (*sollemnis* not *solennis*, *umquam* not *unquam*, *littera* not *litera*, *immo* not *imo*, *auctoritas* not *autoritas*). And I have consistently spelled *respublica* as one word.

Conring uses roman numerals followed by a period to number the chapters or theses into which the *New Discourse* is divided. He also uses them in numbering rulers (e.g., *Gregorius VII.*, *Henricus IV.*, and *Fridericus III.*). He uses arabic numerals followed by a period for numbering years (e.g., *ad annum 769.*, *anno 962.*) and the chapters, books, and other subdivisions of the works to which he refers (e.g., *capitulo 33. distinctione 63.*, or *libro 5. decadum 2.*). I have followed his practice because it seemed reasonable. I have also followed him when he made what seemed to be a significant exception, for example, by using roman numerals for the year of Charlemagne's coronation *anno DCCC.* in chapter seventeen.

Concerning capitalization, Conring used capital letters to signal a plethora of important words or titles and the corresponding adjectives (e.g., *Respublica, Imperium Occidentalis, Imperium Orientalis, Imperator, Caesar, Caesareus, Augustus, Augusteus, Dux, Exarchus, Rex, Regius, Patricius, Pontifex, Papa, Ius Naturae, Ius Gentium, Iurisconsultus, Evangelium, Evangelista, Servator, Deus*). I have removed capitals in all of these cases. I have preserved them only for the names and epithets of individuals and geographical regions (e.g., *Augustus* when used as the name of the founder of the Roman empire, *Lucas, Carolus Magnus, Henricus Auceps, Roma, Romanus, Germania, Pannonia*).

I have expanded all abbreviations (e.g., *libro* not *l.* or *lib.*, *capitulo* not *c.* or *cap.*, *lege* not *l.*, and *et* not *&*). This applies especially to abbreviations in the titles of the books to which Conring refers (e.g., *de translatione imperii Romani* not *de translat. Imper. Rom.*, and *libro de antiquitate reipublicae Batavicae* not *lib. d. antiq. Reipub. Batavicae*).

Italics deserve a bit more explanation. Conring used italics rather consistently for three different purposes. First, he used them in order to highlight direct quotations from other sources (e.g. "Petronii illud: *Orbem iam totum victor Romanus habebat*"). Second, he used them to highlight references to the titles of printed books (e.g., "Hugo Grotius, *de iure belli ac pacis*"), or to the parts of such books (e.g. "teste Zosimo *libro 2.*"), including the number of a year in books arranged according to years, such as the *Annals* of Baronius and the Frankish Annals (e.g., "apud Baronium *ad annum 775.*" and "Annales Francorum *anno 774.*"). Third, he used italics to highlight some of his own conclusions (e.g., in chapter forty-two, "nihil est, cur non aperte tandem pronunciemus, *neque Germaniam neque Langobardicum Italiae regnum vere partes esse Romani imperii*").

In Conring's mind, italics were evidently intended to establish a clear line of typographical demarcation between the prose of his own argument and words that deserved to be set apart from it for one of two reasons: either because they were the words of *other authors* (or at least referred to the *sources* in which such words could be found); or because they embodied *conclusions* that differed from the prose of Conring's argument in the same way in which a theorem differs from the axioms from which it is derived. Perhaps those two reasons can even be reduced to one. For both the quotations from other authors and Conring's conclusions were portable, as it were, separable from the surrounding text, as opposed to that surrounding text itself. It was this distinction that the italics signified. *Quotations* from other authors were put in italics because they had already been exported from their original location and imported into Conring's text. *Conclusions* were italicized because they were supposed to be exported into different contexts. Once their truth had been demonstrated, they no longer needed the support of arguments that had been written (in plain type) only to demonstrate their truth. They were the fruit. The text was the tree on which they grew. They were meant to be plucked off that tree, carried to other destinations, and placed into other contexts, like so many apples ready to be eaten or to be sold at market.

Conring's use of italics, therefore, is more than a purely practical device that makes common sense or helps to avoid confusion. It signals the significance that Conring attributed to *authorship* (his own and that of others) and *authority* (his own and that of his conclusions). He thought it was as important to distinguish his own work from the work of *others* as it was to distinguish the *truth* of his conclusions from the means by which he arrived at them, and he used *italics* for the purpose. That may even help to explain the single occasion on which he used something other than italics as a typographical device for emphasis. At the end of chapter seventeen, he used small capitals to highlight the title ROMANORUM IMPERATOR AUGUSTUS. Why not italics? Perhaps because the title of the Roman emperor was neither a quotation nor a conclusion. For all of these reasons I have made no changes to Conring's use of italics except to regularize it in the few cases in which he himself was not consistent.

A few points deserve special mention. When Conring inserts some words of his own into the italicized text of a quotation from another source, he makes doubly sure that his words will not be confused with the words of his source: he puts his own words in roman type, and on top of that he encloses them in parentheses. This may seem excessive, but it proves to be very necessary when Conring inserts an explanatory comment into a quoted passage that is itself enclosed in parentheses, as for example in this quotation from Otto of Freising in chapter forty-two: "Otto Frisingensis . . . ita loquitur *libro 5. capitulo 35: ex hinc diviso regno regna modo duo orientale et occidentale (quorum alterum* (orientale) *partem Ludovici ac Lotharii . . . aliud vero* (occidentale) *. . . partem Caroli tenet) inveniuntur.* Unde perspicere est . . ." I have followed him in this regard.

Conring vacillates on italicizing references to the Frankish Annals. Sometimes he uses italics (*"Annales Francici"*), most often he does not ("Annales Francici"). This is most likely because the Frankish Annals were a peculiar kind of source. On the one hand, they obviously were a source of quotations formulated by someone other than Conring himself. Hence they deserved italics. Yet on the other hand they could not be attributed to a definite author, nor did Conring refer to a specific printed edition. Hence they did not deserve italics. The solution to this particular problem of confused authority that Conring adopted most of the time was not to italicize, but to use capitals instead: "Annales Francici." I have adopted this as the norm and removed the exceptions.

Conring is similarly inconsistent in italicizing *ad annum* in references to Baronius's *Annals*. Here the inconsistency arose from Baronius's reliance on a measure of time to divide his book into sections. Sometimes the emphasis was on the year as a measure of time. In those cases there was no reason to italicize. Sometimes the emphasis was on the part of Baronius's book that corresponded to that year. In those cases there was every reason to italicize. And sometimes it was impossible to separate one usage from the other. In those cases there was confusion. For the sake of consistency, I have used italics in all cases in which *annus* refers to Baronius's *Annals*.

I have used the footnotes to point out significant variants in the two other versions of the *New Discourse* on which this edition is based: the original academic exercise over which Conring presided in 1641, published in Helmstedt in the same year under the title *Exercitatio de imperatore Romano Germanico*; and the revised version that Conring himself published in Helmstedt in 1674. By significant variants I mean such as affect the meaning of the text or cast light on the relationship between the different editions. I have silently corrected occasional typographical errors and I have paid no heed to mere variations in punctuation, spelling, and typography. Readers may rest assured that, though such differences do exist, they will strike anyone examining the three different versions side by side with less force than the similarities concerning even pure matters of appearance. On a few occasions I have also pointed readers to important but unacknowledged parallels in Hugo Grotius, *De iure belli ac pacis*. All other pertinent information (such as bibliographical data) will be found in the footnotes to the English text, the introduction, the guide to further reading, and the list of works cited in the *New Discourse*.

Abbreviations

1641	Hermann Conring. *Exercitatio de imperatore Romano Germanico.* Respondent Bogislaus Otho von Hoym. Helmstedt: H. Müller, 1641.
New Discourse	Hermann Conring. *Discursus novus de imperatore Romano-Germanico.* N. p., 1642.
1674	Hermann Conring. "De imperatore Romano Germanico." In Hermann Conring, *Exercitationes academicae de republica imperii Germanici infinitis locis mutatae et auctae, inque unum volumen redactae,* 32–72. Helmstedt: Typis Jacobi Mulleri, impensis J. Bartholdi Oehlers, Bibliopolae Lipsiensis, 1674. Repr. in *Opera,* 1:528–42.
Beiträge	Michael Stolleis, ed. *Hermann Conring, 1606–1681: Beiträge zu Leben und Werk.* Historische Forschungen 23. Berlin: Duncker & Humblot, 1983.
Opera	Hermann Conring. *Opera.* Ed. Johann Wilhelm Goebel. 7 vols. Brunswick: Meyer, 1730. Repr. Aalen: Scientia, 1970–1973.
PL	Jacques-Paul Migne, ed. *Patrologiae cursus completus, series Latina.* 221 vols. Paris: Migne, 1844–1902.

Hermann Conring's

New Discourse on the Roman-German Emperor

Discursus novus de imperatore Romano-Germanico

I.[i] Cum aliis multis magistratibus geritur imperium Germanicum, tum unus summus illi praeest, quem caesareum aut regium appellare est moris. Possunt autem de illo multa dici ac varia. Nos vero non nisi pauca nunc attingemus.

II. Atque initio quidem videbimus, quo iure quave iniuria illi competat nomen caesareum et titulus Romanorum imperatoris. Constat quippe illis nominibus appellatos olim, qui imperio Romano regia auctoritate praefuerunt. Ceterum an idem nomen iis, qui Germaniae sociisque regnis praesunt, regibus conveniat, id vero haud perinde liquidum est.

III. Verum hanc quaestionem agitare fortassis haud licebit, nisi et illud agitetur, supersitne hodieque respublica aliqua Romana aut, si non supersit, iura ne eius imperii una cum republica exspiraverint an vero maneant et, si manent, penes quem ergo vere resideant.

IV. Et quidem superesse hodieque Romanum imperium, eiusque nobilissimam portionem esse Germaniam et Italiae pleraque, vulgata adeo est sententia, ut ea de re dubitare videatur merito absurdum et absonum. Quoniam tamen plane contra senserunt nostro saeculo nonnulli ex eruditissimis, resque difficultate non caret, et tamen operae pretium est in re tam magni momenti a veritate non aberrare, non abs re fuerit totum hoc negotium accurate agitare.

V. Principio autem sciendum est, quid olim florentibus Romanorum rebus ad Romanum imperium pertinuerit, sive reapse sive iure. Neque enim desunt nonnulli magni nominis viri, qui totum terrarum orbem Romanis olim paruisse,

---

[i] 1641, 1674: "Thesis I."

New Discourse on the Roman-German Emperor

[A. The issue]

I. The German empire is governed by many magistrates, but only one among them is supreme. By custom we refer to him as "Caesar" or "king." Much could be said about this magistrate, but we are going to limit ourselves to a few points.

II. First we shall consider by what right—or, perhaps, what wrong—the name "Caesar" and the title "emperor of the Romans" belong to him. The magistrates who ruled the Roman empire with the authority of kings in ancient times were obviously called that way. But it is not at all obvious that the same title also belongs to the kings who govern Germany and its associated kingdoms in the present.[1]

III. We cannot explore this issue properly, however, unless we deal with the following questions as well: does the Roman state continue to exist today? If not, did the rights of the Roman empire expire together with the Roman state or did they continue to exist thereafter? And if they did continue to exist thereafter, who really holds them at present?[2]

IV. Now it may well seem absurd to throw any doubt on a view as widely held as that the Roman empire does in fact continue to exist today and that its noblest regions consist of Germany and the greater part of Italy. But some of the most educated men of our times think plainly otherwise. Besides, the subject does not lack its complications, and in a matter of such moment the truth is worth identifying with precision. We do thus seem to have good reason to study this entire issue in detail.

[B. What was the extent of the Roman empire in antiquity?]

V. First of all we need to know what actually or legally belonged to the Roman empire at the time when Rome was flourishing. For there are famous men who declare that the entire world once obeyed the Romans, or should at least have

---

[1] This is the subject of chaps. 5–47.
[2] This is the subject of chaps. 48–56.

vel certe parere debuisse, profiteantur. Usque adeo enim verum id esse, ut alios nunc taceam, credidit olim magnum illud iurisconsultorum lumen Bartolus, ut non dubitaverit adversam sententiam haereseos postulare.

VI. Fundamentum autem opinionis huius peti solet partim ex illis Lucae evangelistae verbis: *exiit edictum a caesare Augusto, ut totus orbis censeretur,* ubi οἰκουμένης voce ambitus imperii Romani circumscribitur; partim ex corpore iuris Iustinianeo, ubi persaepe imperatori *orbis* dominium tribuitur; partim denique ex iis quae apud alios scriptores legas, quale est Petronii illud:

Orbem iam totum victor Romanus habebat,

et Dionysii Halicarnassei *libro 1. capitulo 3.: Romanorum civitas imperat per cunctas terrae plagas, quae quidem inaccessae non sunt, sed habitantur ab hominibus.*[ii]

VII. Verumenimvero totum terrarum orbem paruisse aliquando Romano populo aut eius caesaribus, id vero ita repugnat historicis monumentis, ut hodie in tanta litterarum luce id asserere vel indocti hominis fuerit vel impudentis.

[ii] Compare the unacknowledged parallel in Hugo Grotius, *De iure belli ac pacis*, bk. 2, chap. 22, sec. 13, ed. James Brown Scott, 2 vols. (Washington, DC: Carnegie Institution, 1913–1925), 1:387.

obeyed them. Bartolus himself, the great luminary of jurisconsults, not to mention anybody else, was so certain of this truth that he did not hesitate to brand conflicting views as heresy.³

VI. Usually this opinion is buttressed by quoting from the gospel of Luke that "there went out a decree from Caesar Augustus that all the world should be taxed,"⁴ where the extent of the Roman empire is defined as the whole world,⁵ or from the Justinianic *Corpus Iuris*, where dominion over the world is often attributed to the emperor,⁶ or, finally, from ancient writers like Petronius, who said that "the Roman conqueror now held the whole world,"⁷ and Dionysius of Halicarnassus, book one, chapter three, according to whom "the city of the Romans rules all quarters of the earth—or those at least which are accessible and inhabited by human beings."⁸

VII. Nonetheless the opinion that the entire world once obeyed the Roman people or its emperors is in such blatant conflict with historical records that, given the bright light spread by letters nowadays, it could be maintained only by the unlearned or the impudent.

---

³ Bartolus on *Digesta* 49.15.24 and on *Digesta* 2.1.1. See Bartolus of Sassoferrato, *Opera*, 12 vols. (Venetiis: Apud Iuntas, 1570–1571), 6:228 and 1:47. For an early modern edition of the passages on which Bartolus commented see *Corpus iuris civilis in quatuor partes distinctum*, ed. Dionysius Gothofredus (Francofurti ad Moenum: Sumptibus Societatis, typis B. C. Wustii sen., 1688). For the critical edition see *Digesta*, ed. Theodor Mommsen, vol. 1 of *Corpus Iuris Civilis* (Berlin: Weidmann, 1872). Cf. *The Digest of Justinian*, trans. Alan Watson, 4 vols. (Philadelphia: University of Pennsylvania Press, 1985).

⁴ Luke 2:1.

⁵ Conring uses the Greek οἰκουμένη.

⁶ Actually it is rather difficult to find any passages in Roman law where the emperor explicitly claims dominion over the world. But in *Digesta* 14.2.9 he certainly does call himself "lord of the world" (*mundi dominus*). Cf. the preamble to the *Institutes*, the constitution *Omnem* introducing the *Digesta*, *Codex* 1.1.1, and *Codex* 7.37.3.

⁷ Petronius Arbiter, *Satyricon*, chap. 119, trans. Michael Heseltine, rev. E. H. Warmington, Loeb Classical Library (Cambridge, MA: Harvard University Press, 1975), 252–53.

⁸ *The Roman Antiquities of Dionysius of Halicarnassus*, trans. Earnest Cary, 7 vols., Loeb Classical Library (Cambridge, MA: Harvard University Press, 1937–1950), 1:10–11. Except for the concluding quotation from Dionysius of Halicarnassus, the quotations in this chapter are almost certainly borrowed from Hugo Grotius, *De iure belli ac pacis*, bk. 2, chap. 22, sec. 13, ed. Scott, trans. Kelsey, 2:551–52.

VIII. Etenim constat quidem ex historiis late patuisse terminos Romani imperii cumprimis imperatore Traiano. Certum vero est, ne Europam quidem integram, multo minus Asiae et Africae (nam de America ignota tunc prorsus terra ne verbulum quidem addam) universa finibus illis tum fuisse comprehensa. Quod ex veterum monumentis cum ab aliis, tum a Iusto Lipsio *libro 1. admirandorum sive de magnitudine Romana capitulo 3.* et Onuphrio Panvinio *libro 3. commentariorum de republica Romana* praeclare est expositum. Et quidem imprimis notatu dignum hic est, Germaniam nostram, quae trans Rhenum et Danubium Romanis erat, bellum quidem perpetuum cum Romanis per aliquot saecula a Iulii Caesaris usque temporibus gessisse, numquam tamen in provinciam fuisse a Romanis redactam, sed ex adverso Germanos tandem hostibus suis Romanis pleraque, quae sive in Europa sive in Africa tenuerunt, iure belli eripuisse. Quin immo ne quidem omnes Germani qui cis Rhenum vixerunt, adeoque portio Romani imperii veteris olim sunt habiti, omni ex parte Romanis fuere subiecti, sed nonnulli cum iis tantum societatem coluerunt, fratres Romanorum ideo dicti. Quod de Batavis insulam Rheni habitantibus diserte testatur Tacitus *libro de moribus*

[B.a. The extent of the ancient Roman empire in fact]

VIII. Historical writings certainly establish that the boundaries of the Roman empire extended very far indeed, especially under Emperor Trajan. But it is also certain that they did not include all of Europe, much less all of Asia and Africa—and I am not even going to say a word about America, which was entirely unknown at the time. This has been clearly demonstrated from ancient records by, among others, Justus Lipsius, *Admiranda or the Greatness of Rome*, book one, chapter three,[9] and Onofrio Panvinio, *Commentaries on the Roman Republic*, book three.[10]

In the present context it is especially worth noting that for several centuries after the times of Julius Caesar our Germany, which lay on the opposite side of the Rhine and the Danube from the Romans, fought almost perpetually against the Romans, but was never turned into a Roman province. On the contrary, in the end the Germans took by right of conquest most of the land their Roman enemies had held in Europe and Africa. Indeed, not even all of the Germans who lived on the Roman side of the Rhine were regarded as an integral part of the ancient Roman empire, subject to the Romans in every respect. Some of them entered only into an alliance with the Romans and were therefore called "brothers" of the Romans. Tacitus in his *Germania*[11] and in his *Histories*, book four,[12] says this

---

[9] Justus Lipsius, *Admiranda, sive de magnitudine Romana libri quattuor*, 2nd ed. (Antverpiae: Ex officina Plantiniana, apud Ioannem Moretum, 1599).

[10] Onofrio Panvinio, *Reipublicae Romanae commentariorum libri tres* (Venetiis: Ex officina Erasmiana apud V. Valgrisium, 1558). The statements by Onofrio Panvinio in which Conring was presumably most interested can be found on pp. 663–86, where the growth of Rome is described in general; 763–807, where Roman provinces outside of Italy are described; and especially 844–45, listing the eastern provinces conquered by Trajan. Panvinio himself, however, stated (667) that Rome managed to extend its empire "over the entire world" (*totius orbis terrarum imperium*) and referred to Dionysius of Halicarnassus and Tacitus as sources of information about the customs and institutions enabling it to do so—the opposite of Conring's point. That is hardly an accident. Conring seems to have derived mischievous pleasure from making his point by quoting the writings of authors who maintained the opposite of his. For another example, see his reference to Bellarmine, below, p. 37 nn. 72, 73. He clearly knew how to exploit what is now sometimes referred to as the difference between locutionary content and illocutionary act.

[11] Tacitus, *Germania*, chap. 29. See Tacitus, *Dialogus, Agricola, Germania*, trans. William Peterson and Maurice Hutton, Loeb Classical Library (London: Heinemann, 1914), 304.

[12] Tacitus, *Histories*, bk. 4, chap. 12. See Tacitus, *The Histories. The Annals*, trans. Clifford H. Moore, 4 vols., Loeb Classical Library (London: Heinemann, 1925–1937), 2:20–23.

Germanorum et *4. Historia,* docte vero deducit Hugo Grotius *libro de antiquitate reipublicae Batavicae capitulo 2.*

IX. Alias vero notissimum quoque est, quae Romani imperii finibus conclusa olim sunt, diverso plane titulo ad illud imperium pertinuisse. Fuerunt enim coloniae, fuerunt urbes, aut populi foederati, fuerunt socii, fuerunt amici, fuerunt vere subditi et in provinciam redacti, quorum profecto conditio fuit diversissima, etsi tandem per iniuriam socii, foederati, amici, subditi uno paene loco haberentur. Hoc vero discrimen in Italia imprimis olim fuisse observatum, cum ex veterum monumentis vel leviter intuenti perspicuum esse potest, tum exacte traditur a Carolo Sigonio *de antiquo iure Italiae.* Observatum autem fuisse et in Galliis, notius est quam ut egeat probatione. Alibi vero itidem id observatum fuisse, vel unus Plinius docuerit *libro 3. 4. 5. et 6. naturalis historiae,* ubi studiose omnia isthaec discrimina recenset.

X. Nequaquam itaque veram esse Bartoli et aliorum assertionem, quasi Augusti aevo totus terrarum orbis in ditione Romanorum fuerit, manifestum est. Nec vero illa adducta ex evangelio, aut quae in eam sententiam in libris iuris Romani habentur vel alibi leguntur, id quod Bartolus vult evincunt. Subesse enim quandam αὔξησιν etiam ipsis sacris litteris non infrequentem, per se liquet iamque tum a doctissimis est viris animadversum.

expressly about the Batavians who lived on the island of the Rhine,[13] and Hugo Grotius deduced it learnedly in *The Batavian Republic in Antiquity*, chapter two.[14]

IX. It is also important to remember that the areas enclosed within the borders of the Roman empire belonged to the empire on different legal grounds. Besides those that were genuinely subjected and turned into Roman provinces, there were also colonies, confederated cities and peoples, allies, and friends. These differed considerably from each other in their condition, even though in the long run allies, confederates, friends, and subjects were considered, wrongly, to be almost the same. That these distinctions were observed particularly carefully in Italy should be obvious to anyone who inspects the records of antiquity even cursorily, and it is treated with precision by Carlo Sigonio, *The Ancient Law of Italy*.[15] That the same distinctions were also observed in Gaul is too well known to require further proof. And Pliny's *Natural History*, books three, four, five, and six,[16] where all of these distinctions are carefully reviewed, is all by itself sufficient to show that the same distinctions were observed elsewhere as well.

X. The assertion of Bartolus and others that in the age of Augustus the entire world was subject to the Romans is therefore manifestly false. Neither the passages in the Gospel nor those in the books of Roman law or those found elsewhere in support of that view prove what Bartolus wants. For it is evident in itself and has long since been pointed out by the best scholars that even the Bible sometimes exaggerates.

---

[13] The *Insula Batavorum*, also known as *Batavia*, *Betuwe*, or *Beturve*, was not so much an island as a territory about sixty miles in length that was bordered by the Rhine in the north and the Waal in the south. See Tacitus, *The Histories. The Annals*, trans. Moore, 2:22, note 2.

[14] Hugo Grotius, *Liber de antiquitate reipublicae Batavicae* (Lugduni Batavorum: Ex officina Plantiniana Raphelengij, 1610). The reference to chap. 2, "Quae Batavorum respublica fuerit condita primum gente" (how the Batavian commonwealth was originally designed) is incorrect. The reference must be to chap. 3, "Quae Batavorum respublica fuerit florente imperio Romano" (the Batavian commonwealth at the time of the Roman empire) where Grotius points out on p. xxiii that ancient inscriptions "gentem Batavorum, et cives Batavos, non socios, ut hactenus appellati, sed fratres et amicos vocant, tum populi, tum imperii Romani" (ancient inscriptions call the Batavian nation and citizens, not allies, as heretofore, but brothers and friends of the Roman people and empire).

[15] Carlo Sigonio, *De antiquo iure Italiae libri tres ad senatum populumque Romanum*, 2nd ed. (Venetiis: Apud Iordanum Ziletum, 1562), passim.

[16] C. Plinius Secundus, *Natural History*, trans. H. Rackham and W. H. S. Jones, 10 vols., Loeb Classical Library (Cambridge, MA: Harvard University Press, 1938–1963), bks. 3, 4, 5, 6 are 2:2–501.

XI. Non tantum vero totus orbis paruit numquam Romanis, sed ne quidem ad illos ius aliquod imperii in totum orbem pertinuit. Neque enim vel iure divino arbitrario, vel iure naturae ac gentium, vel denique iure civili huiusmodi quid est constitutum. Sane de iure divino arbitrario hinc patet, quoniam tale ius divinum nullibi legitur in sacris voluminibus, nec traditione ad nos devenit, quo uno tamen modo arbitraria dei instituta nobis innotescunt. Tale item ius naturae aut gentium nemo hominum ex principiis natura notis hactenus probavit vel probare conatus est, nec probari videtur posse. Non aliunde tamen ius naturae solet probari. Iure porro civili urbis Romae non potuisse Romanis ius aliquod competere in terrarum orbem, vel puero liquet. Qui enim totum terrarum orbem obliget, quod unus populus sua in urbe constituit?

XII. Ex his vero consequens est, quicquid populus Romanus olim possedit aut imperio suo continuit vel continere debuit, ad id non alios titulos aut alia iura potuisse adhiberi, quam quibus vulgo iure acquiri aliquid aut possideri solet. Neque vero vel ipsi Romani alia olim iura allegarunt quam vel derelicti occupationem, vel ius belli, aut foederis, vel donationem ac similia. Divinum sane aliquod in omnes gentes ius numquam praetextum ab iis est, quale quid tamen videmus a Muhammede iactatum, vere autem pertinuit ad Hebraeos in ea quae commodato ab Aegyptiis acceperant et terram Cananicam.

XIII. Quod si vero illi usitati tituli acquirendi aliquid aut possidendi apud Romanos valuerunt, manifestum quoque est, iisdem titulis potuisse Romanos occupata et possessa iterum amittere adeoque, si quae similibus titulis Romanis erepta nunc ab aliis possidentur, ea non minus iure atque legitimo titulo possideri, atque olim a Romanis possessa sunt.

[B.b. The extent of the ancient Roman empire in law]

XI. But not only did the world never obey the Romans in fact; the Romans also never had any right to rule the world. Nothing of the kind was ever established by a positive law of God, by a law of nature and nations, or by a civil law. This is obviously true for divine positive law, for Sacred Scripture contains no such positive law of God nor has any been transmitted to us by tradition. Yet this is the only way we can know about positive institutions founded on God's free will. Likewise, no one has ever deduced, or tried to deduce, any such law of nature from the known principles of nature, nor does such a deduction seem possible. Yet there is no other source from which the laws of nature are normally derived. And even a child can see that the civil law of the city of Rome could not possibly have given the Romans the right to rule the world, for how could the entire world have been bound by a law that was established by a single people in their city?

XII. It follows that whatever the Roman people once possessed, or ruled, or had the right to rule, cannot have been founded on any other rights or titles than those on which possessions or acquisitions are normally founded. The Romans themselves actually alleged no other rights than those of occupying abandoned land, war, treaty, donation, and so on. They never pretended to have any kind of divine right to rule all nations—the kind of right that we do see being brandished by Mohammed,[17] but that actually belongs to the Hebrews and covers the grant they received from the Egyptians as well as the land of Canaan.

[C. What happened to the Roman empire from antiquity until the times of Charlemagne?]

XIII. But if the Romans justified their acquisitions and possessions on ordinary grounds, they could evidently lose them on the same grounds. Whatever may have been taken from the Romans in this way and is now in the possession of others is therefore secured by titles no less legitimate than those of the Romans.

---

[17] It is unlikely that this mention of Mohammed reflects more than a generic awareness of the universal aspirations of Islam.

XIV. Esse autem Romanis iam ante aliquot saecula primum ea quae ad occidentale imperium, deinde etiam quae ad orientale pertinuerunt, a populis qui Romanis numquam paruere sed, cum essent sui iuris, ab antiquis temporibus bellum cum iis gesserunt erepta, ex historiis notissimum est. Atque in occidentali quidem parte post Theodosium, sub Honorio et Valentiniano III. pauloque post, paene quinquaginta annorum intervallo a Germanicis populis Africae pars maior, Hispania tota, nec non omnes Galliae, Rhetiae, Vindeliciae, Noricum, Pannonia, Britannia ita sunt occupatae, ut post secutis temporibus Romanus populus in illis terris fuerit fere nec visus nec auditus.

XV. Immo regiones illae, ne quidem mussitantibus Romanis, hodieque ab occupatoribus magna ex parte possidentur. Namque ea quidem, quae cis Rhenum sunt ad usque Pyrenaeos montes, Franci ac Burgundi (qui tamen et ipsi a Francis sunt subiugati) iam plus quam mille ducentos annos tenuerunt. Hispaniae etiam a Gothici sanguinis reliquiis hodie regnantur. Britanniam a Romanis relictam Saxones primum, mox Norvegi et Dani[iii] in potestatem suam redegerunt. Vindeliciam et Noricum ad Alpes usque, nec non Rhetiam potissima ex parte, similiter iam plus quam mille centum annos quiete tenent Bavari et Alemanni seu Suevi.

[iii] 1674: "Saxones primum et Angli, mox Dani et Normanni."

[C.a. How the Roman empire was dismantled during the early Middle Ages]

[C.a.i. From Theodosius the Great to Charlemagne]

XIV. Many centuries ago, however, as is perfectly well known from historical writings, the possessions of the western Roman empire and later on those of the eastern empire, too, were conquered by people who had never obeyed the Romans but were legally independent and had fought wars against them since antiquity. In the western empire, following the reign of Theodosius, under Emperors Honorius and Valentinian III and a little beyond, it took German peoples barely fifty years to occupy the greater part of Africa, all of Spain, all of Gaul, Raetia,[18] Vindelicia,[19] Noricum,[20] Pannonia,[21] and Britain so thoroughly that thereafter the Romans were for all practical purposes neither seen nor heard from in any of those lands.

XV. For the most part those regions are still in the possession of the occupiers, without so much as a murmur from the Romans. The Franks and the Burgundians (who were later subjected by the Franks) have held the regions from the Rhine to the Pyrenees for more than twelve hundred years. Descendents of Gothic blood still rule the kingdoms of Spain.[22] The Saxons[23] were the first to take control of Britain after it had been deserted by the Romans, and the Danes and Norwegians[24] followed them later on. The Bavarians and the Alemans, or Swabians, have similarly held Vindelicia and Noricum down to the Alps, as well as the greater part of Raetia, undisturbed for more than a thousand years. The Huns took Pannonia

---

[18] "A Roman province in the Alps, including the Tyrol and parts of Bavaria and Switzerland": *Oxford Latin Dictionary*, ed. P. G. W. Glare (Oxford: Clarendon Press, 1982), 1572.

[19] "The territory of the Vindelici, forming the eastern part of the province of Raetia": *Oxford Latin Dictionary*, 2066.

[20] "A territory (from *c.* 16 B.C., a province) in the Alps south of the Danube roughly corresponding to modern Austria": *Oxford Latin Dictionary*, 1189.

[21] "A Roman province lying to the south and west of the Danube, and north of Dalmatia": *Oxford Latin Dictionary*, 1290.

[22] This should not be taken as anything more than a broad insistence on genealogical continuities from ancient Germanic tribes to their modern descendants. Conring certainly did not consider the Spanish branch of the House of Habsburg to be descended from the Goths.

[23] In the version of 1674 Conring added "and Angles."

[24] In the version of 1674 Conring substituted "Normans" for "Norwegians."

Pannoniam post varias gentes Germanicas Hunni suam fecerunt, quibus Hungari successere, ut tamen hodie magna Pannoniae pars a Germanicis populis Archiducatus Austriae incolis colatur, Hunnis ante octingentos annos a Carolo Magno inde pulsis.

XVI. Quid? Quod ne ipsa quidem Italia in ditione populi Romani aut caesarum permanserit. Nam primum quidem eiecto omni Romanorum praesidio, fixam in illa sedem locavit Odoacer, Herulorum rex. Quo devicto a Theodorico Ostrogothorum rege, tota Italia, ne ipsa quidem urbe Roma excepta, cessit in ditionem (non contradicentibus caesaribus qui Constantinopoli commorabantur) Ostrogothorum regum, qui hac ipsa de causa Italiae reges se appellabant. Quos licet multo post Iustiniani caesaris auspiciis Belisarius et Narses potestate omni exuerint, mox tamen iterum pulso Romanorum praesidio Langobardi, Germanica gens, sed quae diu Pannoniam tenuerat, paene integram Italiam sibi subiecit. Neque enim mansit quicquam Romanorum imperatoribus Constantinopoli degentibus praeter ipsam urbem Romam, eiusque pomoeria, Pentapolim item, nec non exarchatum Ravennatensem, Venetiarum urbem, et Calabriam. Quin et horum pleraque ultimi Langobardorum reges, Aistulphus imprimis, occuparunt. Non enim quicquam in Italia tandem Langobardis non paruit, praeter urbem Venetam et ultima Calabriae.[iv] Nec tamen vel Venetiae tum amplius Romanorum caesaribus obtemperarunt, sed in libertatem se iam adseruerunt. Quomodo ipsa urbs Roma ultimis illis Langobardorum temporibus caesaris, qui Constantinopoli degebat,

---

[iv] 1674: "praeter Romam, Venetias, et ultima Calabriae."

in the wake of various Germanic tribes, and the Hungarians followed in their train—although there is a large part of Pannonia that is now cultivated by German people from the Archduchy of Austria because Charlemagne expelled the Hungarians from it eight hundred years ago.

XVI. Is it not true that Italy itself did not remain under the sway of the Roman people or its emperors? For the first to establish a fixed seat in Italy after all of the Roman garrisons had been ejected was Odoacer, king of the Herules. When he was defeated by Theodoric, king of the Ostrogoths, all of Italy, including the city of Rome, fell to the kings of the Ostrogoths, who therefore called themselves kings of Italy—without any protest from the emperors residing in Constantinople. To be sure, much later Belisarius and Narses did deprive the Ostrogoths of their power under the auspices of Emperor Justinian. But soon after that the Roman garrisons were expelled once again and the Lombards, a German nation, but one that had occupied Pannonia for a long time, subjected almost all of Italy to their power.

There was then nothing left to the Roman emperors residing in Constantinople except the city of Rome, Rome's immediate vicinity,[25] the Pentapolis,[26] the exarchate of Ravenna,[27] the city of Venice, and Calabria. And most of that, too, was seized by the last kings of the Lombards, especially by Aistulf. For eventually every part of Italy obeyed the Lombards except for the city of Venice[28] and the tip of Calabria. By that time, however, Venice no longer obeyed the Roman emperors either, but insisted on its liberty. And during the final years of Lombard rule the city of Rome itself rejected the emperors of Constantinople.

---

[25] The *pomerium*: "The territory of Rome within the original boundaries (walls) of the city": A. Berger, *Encyclopedic Dictionary of Roman Law* (Philadelphia: American Philosophical Society, 1953), 635.

[26] The Pentapolis consisted of the five coastal cities of Rimini, Pesaro, Fano, Sinigaglia, and Ancona.

[27] An exarchate was a district governed by an exarch. Exarchs were officials of the Byzantine empire who "united civilian and military authority in their respective jurisdictions." From the Byzantine point of view the exarchate of Ravenna included "parts of Liguria, Venetia, Istria, Aemilia, Pentapolis, the duchy of Rome, Perugia, Naples, Calabria, and Apulia, even though not all of these were contiguous, after the loss of Byzantine control of much Italian territory to the Lombards": W. E. Kaegi, "Exarchate," in *Dictionary of the Middle Ages*, ed. Joseph R. Strayer, 13 vols. (New York: Charles Scribner's Sons, 1982–1989), 4:529–30; cf. also A. Kazhdan, "Exarchate," in *Oxford Dictionary of Byzantium*, ed. idem, 3 vols. (New York: Oxford University Press, 1991), 2:767.

[28] In the version of 1674 Conring added "Rome" before "Venice."

imperium detrectabat. Pipinus quidem Francorum rex, Aistulpho devicto, expulit iterum Langobardos exarchatu Ravennatensi nec non Pentapoli (Romano pontifici terris illis attributis, quod persuasus esset ad S. Petri illas patrimonium pertinere), sed reliqua Italiae Langobardis iterum reddidit, ut iuste ab illis possessa. Eius quoque filius Carolus, cognomento Magnus, Desiderio ultimo Langobardorum rege pulso, non dubitavit anno DCCLXXIV. post natum servatorem omne quod in Italia hactenus Langobardi possederant in suam ditionem redigere, Constantinopolitano imperatori aut Romano pontifici vel populo nihil praeter pauca isthaec, Calabriam nempe et quae Pipinus pater Romano pontifici donaverat, relictis. Tantum autem abest, ut id a quoquam fuerit improbatum, ut contra et Romanus pontifex hoc nomine Carolum laudibus in caelum paene extulerit et Constantinopolitani imperatores neutiquam contradixerint, Carolo interim se Francorum ac Langobardorum regem appellante.

XVII. Haec sane facies fuit provinciarum Romani imperii occidentalis, cum Carolus ille Magnus anno DCCC. Romam religionis ergo profectus insperato in aede sacra a Leone pontifice et civibus Romanis festiva acclamatione salutatus est ROMANORUM IMPERATOR AUGUSTUS.

XVIII. Ex his vero constat, ea quidem tempestate Romano populo aut eius pontifici vel caesari nihil iuris fuisse in Germaniam quidem, quae Rheno et Danubio cingitur, utpote quae Romanis paruit numquam. Non minus vero evidens est propemodum, tum quidem Romanis nihil amplius iuris fuisse in Hispaniam, Galliam, Noricum, Vindeliciam, Rhetiam, immo ipsam Italiam, quantum certe eius a Iustiniani aevo possederunt Langobardi. Nam ut nunc non disputem, iure an iniuria provinciae illae a Germanicis populis fuerint occupatae, immo ut verum sit, nonnullas per iniuriam occupatas (sicuti haud fortasse difficile fuerit ostensu, nonnullas iure Romanis ereptas esse), quin tamen postea procedente tempore usucapio iusta et praescriptio intercesserit, negari temere non potest. Neque vero quod dicitur, *quae ab initio non valent ex post facto convalescere non posse,* simpliciter verum est, sed tum demum, si causa nova ius per se parere idonea non accesserit.[v]

---

[v] Cf. Grotius, *De iure belli ac pacis,* bk. 2, chap. 4, sec. 11, ed. Scott, 1:142: "Nam quod dicitur, quae ab initio non valent, ex post facto convalescere non posse, hanc habet exceptionem, nisi causa nova ius per se parere idonea intercesserit."

After his defeat of King Aistulf, Pipin, king of the Franks, expelled the Lombards from the exarchate of Ravenna and the Pentapolis and granted these lands to the bishop of Rome, because he had been persuaded that they belonged to the patrimony of St. Peter. But he returned the rest of Italy to the Lombards as their rightful possession. And when his son Charles, surnamed the Great, had beaten Desiderius, the last king of the Lombards, he did not hesitate to subject all of the Lombard possessions in Italy to his own control in 774, leaving nothing to the emperor of Constantinople, the bishop of Rome, or the people of Rome except a small area, namely, Calabria and what his father Pipin had donated to the bishop of Rome. Far from protesting, the bishop of Rome praised Charles for this very reason almost to high heaven, and the emperors of Constantinople raised no objections at all. Charles, meanwhile, called himself king of the Franks and Lombards.

XVII. This, then, was the extent of the provinces of the western Roman empire in the year eight hundred when Charlemagne went to Rome for religious reasons and, to his surprise, Pope Leo III and the citizens of Rome ceremonially acclaimed him in church as EMPEROR AUGUSTUS OF THE ROMANS.

XVIII. At least at that time, therefore, the people of Rome, their bishop, and their emperor certainly had no rights to Germany on the far side of the Rhine and the Danube, which had never obeyed the Romans in the first place. It is just about equally evident that they had lost their rights to Spain, Gaul, Noricum, Vindelicia, Raetia, and even to the part of Italy that the Lombards had possessed since the times of Justinian. I am not now going to analyze whether German peoples had the right to occupy those provinces or not. I am even prepared to grant that at least in some cases they did not (although it would probably not be difficult to show that in others they did). But it can hardly be denied that with the passage of time these acquisitions fell under rights of usucapion and prescription.[29] For the principle that "what is invalid in the beginning cannot become valid later on" is not unconditionally true, but only if no new reasons come into existence to create new rights.[30]

---

[29] *Usucapio*: "Acquisition of ownership of a thing belonging to another through possession of it (*possessio*) for a period fixed by law"; *Praescriptio longi temporis*: "An institution similar to *usucapio* and applied to provincial land which could not be usucapted under *ius civile*": Berger, *Encyclopedic Dictionary of Roman Law*, 645, 752. Cf. Barry Nicholas, *An Introduction to Roman Law* (Oxford: Clarendon Press, 1962), 120–30.

[30] This sentence is probably quoted from Hugo Grotius, *De iure belli ac pacis*, bk. 2, chap. 4, sec. 11, trans. Kelsey, 2:227. *De iure belli ac pacis*, bk. 2, chap. 4 furnishes the basis for Conring's argument that usucapion and prescription are valid principles of international law. It is explicitly cited below at the end of chap. 20.

XIX. Provincias vero illas quas modo diximus iam isthac aetate pro derelicto habitas a populo Romano, adeoque a possessoribus iure possessas, ex historiis manifestum est. Namque iam supra diximus, per annos ducentos, trecentos populum Romanum illas provincias neque verbis neque factis repetiisse. Quinimmo constat, Romanos cum illis possessoribus, ne Langobardis quidem exceptis, plurimos contractus, tamquam cum legitimis eorum quae possidebant dominis, iniisse. At vero, si is, qui rei alicuius est dominus, sciens cum altero eam rem possidente tamquam cum domino contrahat, ius suum remisisse merito habetur; id quod non tam valet auctoritate iuris civilis Romani, quam ex ipso iure naturae venit.[vi]

XX. Sane de Italia possit quis forte dubitare, propter perpetua fere Constantinopolitanorum caesarum cum Langobardis bella. Sed imprimis observatu dignum est, integram Italiam iam ante concessu et dono Zenonis imperatoris, teste Iornande *libro de rebus Gothicis capitulo 57.*, Ostrogothis cessisse, nec Iustinianum bello suo contra Gothos aliam causam praetexuisse, quam Amaleswentae reginae indignam necem, cuius se vindicem profitebatur. Cum Langobardis postea bella multa quidem gesta, sed etiam multi contractus tamquam cum iustis Italiae dominis sunt initi, manente certamine solum de finibus, non autem de integro regno, quemadmodum ex Pauli Warnefridi *historia Longobardica* probatu est facillimum.

[vi] Cf. Grotius, *De iure belli ac pacis*, bk. 2, chap. 4, sec. 4, ed. Scott, 1:139: "Sic si is qui rei alicuius est dominus, sciens cum altero eam rem possidente, tanquam cum domino contrahat, ius suum remisisse merito habebitur: quod cur non et inter reges locum habeat, et populos liberos nihil causae est. Simile est quod superior concedens inferiori, vel imperans id facere quod facere licite non potest, nisi lege solvatur, lege solvisse eum intelligitur. Venit enim hoc non ex iure civili, sed ex iure naturali, quo quisque suum potest abdicare, et ex naturali praesumtione qua voluisse quis creditur quod sufficienter significavit."

XIX. As early as the age of Charlemagne, in other words, the provinces we have just mentioned were thus considered to have been abandoned by the Roman people and to have entered into the rightful ownership of their possessors. History makes that manifest. As we have pointed out above, the Roman people had failed to reclaim those provinces by words or deeds for two and three hundred years. To the contrary, they had entered into many contracts with the possessors of these provinces, not excepting the Lombards, as with the legitimate owners of what they possessed in fact. But if the legal owner of a certain object enters knowingly into a contract with someone who actually possesses that object as if the possessor were the owner, then the legal owner is properly considered to have surrendered his right—a principle whose validity derives not only from the authority of Roman civil law but from the law of nature itself.[31]

[C.a.ii. The special case of Italy]

XX. There could be some doubt about Italy, however, because the emperors of Constantinople were almost constantly at war with the Lombards. It is therefore worth noting, to begin with, that all of Italy had already yielded to the Ostrogoths when Emperor Zeno granted it to them, witness Jordanes, *Gothic History*, chapter fifty-seven,[32] and that Justinian himself based his war against the Goths on no other reason than the brutal murder of Queen Amalasuntha, on whose behalf he claimed to be taking revenge. It is true that the emperors of Constantinople fought many wars against the Lombards later on. But it is also true that they entered into many contracts with them, as if the Lombards were the rightful owners of those parts of Italy that they controlled in fact. They continued to fight with the Lombards only about the precise location of the boundaries, not their title to the kingdom as a whole, as is easily demonstrable from Paul Warnfried's *History of the Lombards*.[33]

---

[31] The sentence beginning with "But if the legal owner . . ." is probably quoted from Hugo Grotius, *De iure belli ac pacis*, bk. 2, chap. 4, sec. 4, trans. Kelsey, 2:222.

[32] Jordanes, *De origine actibusque Getarum*, ed. Francesco Giunta and Antonino Grillone (Rome: Nella sede dell' istituto Palazzo Borromini, 1991), 119–22. See also *PL* 69:1251–1296, here 1292–1293. Cf. Jordanes, *The Gothic History of Jordanes in English Version*, trans. Charles Christopher Mierow (Princeton: Princeton University Press, 1915), 134–37. For this and the next see Walter Goffart, *The Narrators of Byzantine History (A.D. 550–800): Jordanes, Gregory of Tours, Bede, and Paul the Deacon* (Princeton: Princeton University Press, 1988).

[33] Paulus Diaconus, "Historia Langobardorum," in *Scriptores rerum Langobardicarum et Italicarum saec. VI–IX*, ed. L. Bethmann and G. Waitz, Monumenta Germaniae Historica (Hannover: Hahn, 1878), 12–219. See also *PL* 95:433–672. Cf. Paulus Diaconus, *History of the Langobards*, trans. William Dudley Foulke (New York: Longmans, 1907).

Iam ante vero inculcatum etiam est, totum Langobardorum regnum, devicto Desiderio rege, per triginta ferme annos ante imperatorium titulum acceptum a Carolo Magno, non tantum non reclamantibus verum etiam laudantibus Romanis, fuisse possessum. Atqui vero id, quod derelictum est, iure possideri ab eo, qui tamquam in vacuam venit possessionem, iuris naturae est. Accessit vero et usucapionis et praescriptionis ius, quae non minus naturalem vim habent,[vii] non autem iure tantum civili valent, ut praeclare contra Vasquium disputat Hugo Grotius *libro 2.*[viii] *de iure belli ac pacis capitulo 4.*

XXI. Hic tamen observandum venit, quod iam supra innuimus, etsi Langobardi a Narsete invitati in Italiam penetraverint, numquam tamen omnes eius partes sibi subiecisse, sed mansisse sat magnam Italiae portionem in fide et obsequio imperatorum Romanorum Constantinopoli degentium qui, cum per varios duces, tum vero cumprimis per exarchos Ravennae consistentes, superstites illas imperii Romani reliquias gubernabant. Erat autem exarchus, si Iosepho Scaligero *libro 3. canonum isagogicorum pagina 339.* credimus, *praefecti praetorio vicarius, qui Ravennam cum aliquot urbibus imperii Romani nomine adversus Langobardos tuebatur.* Inter autem eas reliquias fuit ipsa urbs Roma, quam per ducem aliquem Constantinopoli missum caesares regebant. Non est nostrum hoc loco de finibus et superstitibus illis Romani imperii in Italia provinciis agere. Fecit hoc ipsum magna cum cura Eyricius Puteanus singulari opere, quo exarchatus historiam est complexus. Ex eo tamen usque tempore, adeoque statim ab Iustiniani obitu et Langobardorum in Italiam adventu, pars Italiae regni Langobardici, pars antiquo imperii Romani

---

[vii] 1674: "quae ipsissimam naturalem vim habent."
[viii] 1641, 1674: "*libro 1.*"

Moreover, I have already pointed out above that, after he defeated Desiderius, Charlemagne controlled the entire Lombard kingdom for almost thirty years before he accepted the imperial title. During that time the Romans not only failed to reclaim the Lombard kingdom but even gave their approval to Charlemagne's rule. Now it is a law of nature that whatever has been abandoned is rightfully possessed by whoever has occupied it as if it were vacant. The same conclusion is supported by the rights of usucapion and prescription, which have no less natural force[34] and do not derive their validity only from civil law, as Grotius argues with great clarity in *The Law of War and Peace*, book two, chapter four,[35] against Vázquez.[36]

XXI. As was shown above, however, even if Narses did invite the Lombards to enter, they never subjected all of Italy. A considerable part of Italy remained faithful and obedient to the Roman emperors residing in Constantinople, who governed these fragments of the empire through various dukes and above all through the exarchs of Ravenna. If we believe Scaliger, *Introductory Rules*, book three, page 339,[37] the Exarch was "the vicar of the Praetorian Prefect, who protected Ravenna and certain other cities from the Lombards in the name of the Roman empire." Among those fragments of the empire was the city of Rome itself, which the emperors of Constantinople ruled by a duke on special dispatch.

This is not the place for us to deal with the provinces remaining to the Roman empire in Italy or their boundaries. Erycius Puteanus has done so with great care in a remarkable work in which he has included the history of the Exarchate.[38] The point is that from then on, that is, since the death of Justinian and the arrival of the Lombards in Italy, one part of Italy was called the Lombard kingdom

---

[34] In the version of 1674 Conring expressed himself more resolutely by stating that usucapion and prescription "have the force of natural law itself."

[35] Hugo Grotius, *De iure belli ac pacis*, bk. 2, chap. 4, "On Assumed Abandonment of Ownership and Occupation Consequent Thereon; and Wherein this Differs from Ownership by Usucapion and by Prescription," trans. Kelsey, 2:220–30. The *Exercitatio* of 1641 refers to *De iure belli ac pacis*, bk. 1, chap. 4, where Grotius deals with wars by subjects against superiors. That is clearly mistaken. In the *New Discourse* the reference is corrected. The version of 1674 repeats the error of the first version.

[36] Fernando Vázquez Menchaca, *Controversiarum illustrium aliarumque usu frequentium libri tres*, ed. and trans. Fidel Rodriguez Alcalde, 4 vols. (Valladolid: Talleres tip. "Cuesta", 1931–1934).

[37] Joseph Justus Scaliger, *Isagogicorum chronologiae canonum libri tres*, in idem, *Thesaurus temporum* (Lugduni Batavorum: Excudebat Thomas Basson, 1606), 339. I am grateful to Anthony Grafton for help with this reference.

[38] Erycius Puteanus, *Historiae insubricae libri vi, qui irruptiones barbarorum in Italiam continent* (Oxonii: G. Turner, 1634).

cognomento fuit appellata. Atque Langobardici quidem quae erant regni non recuperarunt caesares Constantinopoli habitantes, reliquiae vero illae imperii, urbe Roma et Veneta aliisque pauculis exceptis, pervenerunt tandem cum ipsa urbe Ravenna in Langobardorum ditionem. Illum tamen exarchatum Aistulpho regi expressum, precibus et impie confictis Petri apostoli nomine litteris (quas recitat et laudare non dubitat Baronius *ad annum 755. tomo 9. annalium*) a Stephano papa circumventus, Pipinus S. Petro, id est Romano papae, utut contra niteretur caesaris legatus, donavit. Quam rem late narrat post Anastasium, Annales Francicos, aliosque scriptores Baronius *ad annum 753*.[ix]

XXII. Notatu autem digna sunt verba Baronii loco citato, quando scribit Stephanum papam legatos misisse primum ad Constantinum imperatorem (is est quem Copronymum nuncupant), *ut adversus Langobardos ad defensionem eorum quae supererant imperii Romani in Italiam exercitum mitteret.* Item, *cum nulla spes esset, ut Constantinus imperator iura imperii quae in Italia residua erant a Langobardis invasa defenderet.* Subiicit vero Baronius verba Anastasii, quae docent Stephanum nihil

---

[ix] 1641: "735."

while another continued to be referred to by its old name as Roman empire. Now the emperors of Constantinople failed to recover the Lombard kingdom whereas the Lombards eventually did gain control over the remaining fragments of the Roman empire, including Ravenna and excluding only Rome, Venice, and a few other areas. But when he had seized it from King Aistulf, Pipin donated the Exarchate over the objections of the imperial legate to St. Peter, that is to the Roman pope, because he had been tricked by Pope Stephen's entreaties and the ungodly letters fabricated in the name of the Apostle Peter, which Baronio does not hesitate to cite and approve for the year 755 in his *Annals*, volume nine.[39] Baronio, basing himself on Anastasius,[40] the *Frankish Annals*,[41] and other writers, describes the entire affair in detail for the year 753.[42]

XXII. Here it is worth quoting Baronio directly. He writes for 753 that Pope Stephen first sent legates to Emperor Constantine, also known as Copronymus, "to persuade him to send an army to Italy in order to defend the remnants of the Roman empire from the Lombards." Likewise: "Since there was no hope that Emperor Constantine would defend the remaining rights of the empire in Italy against attack from the Lombards . . ." But Baronio adds words from Anastasius

---

[39] Cesare Baronio, *Annales ecclesiastici [A.D. 1–1565] auctore Caesare Baronio . . . una cum critica historico-chronologica P. Antonii Pagii*, 38 vols. (Lucae: Typis L. Venturini, 1738–1759). In this edition the "ungodly letters" that prompted Pipin to march into Italy appear in vol. 12:615–17. They resulted in the so-called Donation of Pipin, on which see *Dictionary of the Middle Ages*, 9:500–3, s.v. Pepin III.

[40] Anastasius Bibliothecarius, *Historia de vitis Romanorum pontificum* (Moguntiae: In typographeio Ioannis Albini, 1602). See also Louis Duchesne, ed., *Le Liber pontificalis: Texte, introduction et commentaire*, 2nd ed., 3 vols., Bibliothèque des Ecoles Françaises d'Athènes et de Rome, 2nd ser., 3 (Paris: E. de Boccard, 1955–1957), and *PL* 127–128. Cf. *The Book of Pontiffs (Liber pontificalis): The Ancient Biographies of the First Ninety Roman Bishops to A.D. 715*, trans. Raymond Davis (Liverpool: Liverpool University Press, 1989), and *Lives of the Eighth-Century Popes: Liber Pontificalis, 715–817 A.D.*, trans. Raymond Davis (Liverpool: Liverpool University Press, 1992). The *Liber pontificalis* is arranged according to the lives of individual popes. It is no longer attributed to Anastasius.

[41] *Annales regum Francorum* (Coloniae: Ioannes Birckmannus, 1562), year 753. See also "Annales Regni Francorum. Die Reichsannalen," in *Quellen zur Karolingischen Reichsgeschichte. Erster Teil*, ed. and trans. Reinhold Rau (Darmstadt: Wissenschaftliche Buchgesellschaft, 1977), 9–155, and *PL* 104:367–508. Cf. *Carolingian Chronicles: Royal Frankish Annals and Nithard's Histories*, trans. Bernhard Walter Scholz (Ann Arbor: University of Michigan Press, 1970), 35–125.

[42] The *Exercitatio* of 1641 has 735 instead of 753. That is an obvious misprint. It was corrected both in the *New Discourse* and in the version of 1674.

aliud petiisse restitui, quam vicina quaedam castra ex exarchatum Ravennae et Aemiliae oppida a Langobardis occupata. Nec vero aliud reddi sibi petit Stephanus impiis iis et ineptis litteris quas ad Pipinum misit anno 755.[x] et ex Vaticana bibliotheca primus edidit Baronius. Sed nec aliud quidpiam per Pipinum Aistulpho Langobardo est ereptum. Diserte enim Annales Francici: *Pipinus redditam sibi Ravennam et Pentapolim et omnem exarchatum ad Ravennam pertinentem ad S. Petrum tradidit.* Anastasius Bibliothecarius idem prorsus narrat in vita Stephani, simulque enumerat urbes omnes nominatim donatione hac comprehensas. Plura quidem narrat donata Leo Ostiensis *historia Cassinensi libro 2. capitulo 7.*, quem sequitur Baronius. Sed quis homini recentiori contra omnes eius aevi scriptores credat? Restituit autem haec et Carolus Magnus postquam, devicto Desiderio Langobardorum rege, Langobardorum regnum subiugasset. Quinimmo et addidit nonnulla, quae recitat Anastasius in vita Hadriani, ex uno vero hoc recenset Baronius *ad annum 774.* Unde obiter est colligere, novae illius donationis Caroli Magni, ut nec illius Pipinianae, ullum hodie monumentum in scriniis Romanis reperiri, quinimmo ne testimonium quidem eius aliud superesse praeter illud unum Anastasii, et quidem aulae Romanae mancipii. Qua de re nunc latius disserere non licet.

XXIII. Quicquid vero huius sit, id certum est, neque Carolum Magnum Langobardorum regno destructo potiorem istam Italiae partem vel populo Romano vel eius pontifici vel caesari Constantinopolitano concessisse, neque vel populum illum vel pontificem vel caesarem postulasse eam sibi restitui, sed in Francorum ditionem eam omnem terram pervenisse. Certe eius postulati nulla reperitur memoria, multo minus huiusmodi alicuius concessionis. Contra testantur historiae, Carolum Magnum statim a devicto Desiderio regnum Langobardorum omne quasi iure belli occupatum administrasse. Hinc Annales Francorum *anno 774.:*

---

[x] 1674: "855."

which prove that Stephen had asked the emperor only for restitution of certain castles in the vicinity of Rome, the exarchate of Ravenna, and the towns of Emilia that had been occupied by the Lombards. This is exactly the same as what he asked from Pipin in those ungodly and absurd letters that he sent to him in 755,[43] which Baronio was the first to publish from the Vatican Library. Nor did Pipin receive anything other than that from Aistulf the Lombard. The *Frankish Annals* are explicit on this point: "When Ravenna, the Pentapolis, and the whole of the Exarchate that belonged to Ravenna had been returned to Pipin, he transferred them to St. Peter."[44] Anastasius Bibliothecarius tells the same story in his *Life of Stephen* and at the same time lists the cities included in the donation by name. To be sure, Leo of Ostia, *History of Monte Cassino*, book two, chapter seven,[45] claims that there were more gifts than that, and Baronio agrees with him. But who will trust such recent authors more than all the writers contemporary to the events? Charlemagne made exactly the same restitution after he had defeated King Desiderius and subjugated the kingdom of the Lombards. Baronio, for the year 774, maintains that Charlemagne added certain other areas merely because Anastasius lists them in the *Life of Hadrian*. We might therefore note in passing that no historical records of this new donation of Charlemagne or of the donation of Pipin can be found in the Roman archives today, indeed, that there is no independent evidence at all to support the words of Anastasius, who was, after all, a servant of the Roman court. But this is not the time to pursue this issue any further.

XXIII. Whatever the case may be, certain is this: after he had destroyed the kingdom of the Lombards, Charlemagne did not concede the better part of Italy to the Roman people, their bishop, or the emperor of Constantinople, nor did the people, bishop, or emperor request any such restitution. The entire territory came under Frankish rule instead. No record of a contrary request on the part of the Romans can be found anywhere, much less of any corresponding concession. To the contrary, the histories testify that immediately after his defeat of Desiderius Charlemagne administered the whole kingdom of the Lombards himself, as having occupied it by right of war. Thus the *Frankish Annals* for 774: "King Charles returned

---

[43] Baronio, *Annales ecclesiastici*, year 755. The version of 1674 has 855 instead of 755.
[44] *Annales Regum Francorum*, year 756.
[45] Leo Marsicanus, *Chronicon antiquum sacri monasterii Cassinensis* (Neapoli: Ex Typ. T. Longhi, 1616), bk. 1, chap. 8. See also *PL* 173:479–978, here 501. Also in *Die Chronik von Montecassino*, ed. H. Hoffmann, Monumenta Germaniae Historica, Scriptores 34 (Hannover: Hahn, 1980), 35–36. The Italian translation *Cronaca di Montecassino* (III 26–33), ed. F. Aceto and V. Lucherini (Milan: Jaca, 2001), begins at a later point in the text. Conring's reference to bk. 2, chap. 7, may be a misprinted borrowing from Baronio, who refers to bk. 1, chap. 7, in his account of the year 755.

rex Carolus subacta et pro tempore ordinata Italia in Franciam revertitur. Poetaster anonymus antiquus *libro 1. annalium:*

> Dedita tum Francis haec urbs clarissima (Papia scilicet) *cunctis*
> *Exemplo fuerat reliquis. Nam protinus omnes*
> *Tradiderunt Carolo sese concorditer urbes*
> *Eiusdem regni, quod iam sibi iure subactum*
> *Disposuit, quantum potuit pro tempore tali.*

Iidem Annales, ut ille Poetaster, memorant anno 776. Rotgaudum Foroiuliensibus ducem a Carolo datum defecisse, sed illo devicto provinciam istam Francorum comitibus traditam. Anno item 779. ducem Spoletanum in ducatu suo confirmatum. Iidem memorant anno 71.[xi] Pipinum filium Caroli regem Langobardiae esse constitutum. Verba eorundem memoratu digna sunt anno 786: *rex statuit Romam proficisci, et partem Italiae in qua Beneventum situm est aggredi conveniens esse arbitratus, in illius regni residuam portionem cuius caput, capto Desiderio rege, maioremque partem in Langobardia tam subacta tenebat.* Testantur vero iidem etiam Beneventanum ducatum Carolo tunc cessisse, et quidem Adriani pontificis consilio. Mitto alia testimonia, ne videar soli lucem faeneraturus. Id non possum non adducere, Carolum statim a capto Desiderio seipsum regem Francorum et Langobardorum appellasse. Recitat eius epistolam ad Albinum anno 778., item privilegium concessum monasterio Parisiensi S. Vincentii anno 773. hoc titulo ornatum Baronius. Ipse Adrianus papa hoc titulo Carolum laudat longa illa epistola ad Constantinum et Irenen perscripta, quam ex actis concilii Nicaeni secundi recitat idem Baronius *ad annum 785.* Ex quibus perspicuum est, totum Langobardorum regnum tenuisse Carolum, et quidem nullius beneficio sed suo gladio acquisitum. Neque in illud vel populum Romanum, vel pontificem, vel denique caesarem Constantinopolitanum quidquam amplius sibi iuris arrogasse.

[xi] An obvious misprint for 781 that was never corrected in any version of the text.

to France after he had subdued Italy and organized it for the time being."[46] The old anonymous poet puts it similarly in book one of his *Annals*:

> The surrender of that most illustrious city (namely, Pavia) to the Franks became an example for all the rest. Forthwith all the other cities of the kingdom handed themselves over to Charles in unison. Having subjected the kingdom by right, Charles disposed over it as best he could at the time.[47]

The same *Frankish Annals*, like the said poet, report that in 776 Rotgaud, whom Charles had appointed duke of Friuli, defected and that after his defeat the province was transferred to Frankish counts. They also report that in 779 the duke of Spoleto was confirmed in his duchy. And they record that in 71[48] Pipin, the son of Charlemagne, was made king of Lombardy. Their words regarding the year 786 are worth quoting: "The king decided to march to Rome and judged it appropriate to invade the part of Italy where Benevento is situated, that is, the remaining portion of the kingdom whose head he had captured in Desiderius and whose greater part he held in Lombardy." They also testify that the Duchy of Benevento yielded to Charles and did so on the advice of Pope Hadrian.

I shall forego other testimonies lest I shall seem to lend light to the sun. But I cannot resist adding that, immediately after the capture of Desiderius, Charles called himself king of the Franks and Lombards. Baronio quotes his letter to Albinus[49] of 778 as well as the privilege granted to the monastery of St. Vincent in Paris in 773,[50] which is embellished by that title. Pope Hadrian himself honors Charles with this title in that long letter to Constantine and Irene that Baronio quotes for the year 785 from the acts of the second council of Nicaea.[51] That makes it obvious that Charles ruled the entire kingdom of the Lombards and that he acquired it not through anyone's kindness but with his sword, while the Roman people, the Roman bishop, and even the emperor of Constantinople claimed no more rights over it. The same conclusion, finally, is confirmed by the fact that,

---

[46] *Annales Regum Francorum*, year 774.

[47] Poeta Saxo, "Annalium de gestis Caroli Magni imperatoris libri quinque," in *Poetae Latini Aevi Carolini*, ed. Paul von Winterfeld, Monumenta Germaniae Historica (Berlin: Weidmann, 1899), 4:1–71, year 774. See also *PL* 99:683–736, here 689B. Cf. Poeta Saxo, *The Saxon Poet's Life of Charles the Great*, trans. Mary E. McKinney (New York: Pageant Press, 1956), 16.

[48] An obvious misprint that is shared by the *New Discourse* with all versions of the *Exercitatio*. The correct year is 781.

[49] Otherwise known as Alcuin. See Baronio, *Annales ecclesiastici*, year 778.

[50] Another, but not so obvious, error that is shared by the *New Discourse* and all versions of the *Exercitatio*. The correct year is 779. See Baronio, *Annales ecclesiastici*, year 779.

[51] Baronio, *Annales ecclesiastici*, year 785.

Et postremum quidem eo confirmatur, quod (si credimus Baronio) Irene imperatrix ruperit anno 788. sponsalia inter Constantinum et filiam Caroli contracta, quod *Carolus ducatum Beneventanum invasisset, quem in suum patrocinium orientales imperatores susceperant.* De toto scilicet Langobardico regno mota lis nulla fuit.

XXIV. Haec vero cum ita sese habeant, manifestum est id quod supra etiam diximus, eo tempore, quo Carolus imperatoris titulum accepit (contigit illud autem anno 800. ipsis feriis natalitiis), pleraque occidentalis imperii veteris fuisse iamdudum a Carolo possessa, et quidem nullam amplius controversiam de iure possessionis Romanis moventibus. Constat etiam tum temporis neque in Hispania, neque in Galliis, neque in Germania, neque in Pannonia quidquam Romanae amplius fuisse ditionis. Immo ne in Italia quidem quid fuisse reliquum, quod sibi arrogarent Romani, praeter urbem ipsam Romam, exarchatum Ravennatensem, et si quae alia oppida aut Pipinus aut Carolus Langobardis erepta Romano pontifici donaverant.

XXV. Non tantum vero nihil paene possessum tum fuit Romanis in toto occidente, sed et ius omne deperdita recuperandi longo tempore iam exspiraverat. Bene scilicet apud Isocratem Archidemus Messenam repetentibus Thebanis dixit, *possessiones, sive privatas sive publicas, praescriptione longi temporis firmatas in patrimonio et dominio habendas omnibus est persuasum.* Et vero hoc ipso iuxta alia Iephthes iniuriae convincit Ammonitarum regis vendicantis sibi terras inter Arnonem et Iabocum ad Iordanum sitas conatum, ceu legere est *capitulo 11. iudicum commate 26.*[xii]

XXVI. Si autem neque provinciae occidentalis imperii veteris amplius tum in ditione fuerunt Romani populi, immo si nec ius aliquod in illas provincias populus amplius habuit, manifestum est per imperatorium titulum Carolo Magno

---

[xii] Compare the unacknowledged parallels in Grotius, *De iure belli ac pacis*, bk. 2, chap. 4, sec. 2, ed. Scott, 1:138.

if we can believe Baronio, Empress Irene broke the engagement of Constantine with the daughter of Charles in 788 because "Charles had invaded the Duchy of Benevento, which the eastern emperors had taken under their protection."[52] Consequently there was no dispute about the Lombard kingdom as a whole.

[C.a.iii. The Roman empire at the time of Charlemagne's imperial coronation]

XXIV. Given all of this, it is manifestly true, as we have said before,[53] that most parts of the old western Roman empire had long since been in Charles's possession and that the Romans were no longer disputing his right to these possessions when he accepted the imperial title on Christmas day A.D. 800. It is similarly true that no traces of Roman rule were left in Spain, Gaul, Germany, and Pannonia. Even in Italy nothing was left for the emperors to claim except the city of Rome itself, the exarchate of Ravenna, and whichever other cities Pipin or Charles may have donated to the bishop of Rome after taking them from the Lombards.

XXV. Indeed, not only had the Romans lost nearly all of their possessions in the west, but any right of recovering their losses had also expired long ago. It was exactly on this point that Archidamus once gave an excellent answer to the Thebans when they tried to recover Messene, as can be read in Isocrates: "Everyone agrees that both private and public possessions are to be considered the patrimony and property of those to whom they have been confirmed by long-term prescription."[54] And by this very same right, among others, Jephthah proved the injustice of the king of the Ammonites who tried to reclaim the lands on the Jordan between the Arnon and the Jabbok, as can be read in the book of Judges, chapter eleven, verse twenty-six.[55]

[C.b. The meaning of Charlemagne's imperial title]

XXVI. Now, if the provinces of the old western empire were no longer under the control of the Roman people, and their legal right to those provinces had lapsed as well, it obviously follows that the imperial title neither put, nor could

---

[52] Baronio, *Annales ecclesiastici*, year 788.

[53] In chaps. 16–17.

[54] Isocrates, *Archidamus*, chap. 26. See *Isocrates*, trans. George Norlin, 3 vols., Loeb Classical Library (London: Heinemann, 1928–1945), 1:360.

[55] These quotations from Isocrates' *Archidamus* and from the Bible's Book of Judges are probably borrowed from Hugo Grotius, *De iure belli ac pacis*, bk. 2, chap. 4, sec. 2, trans. Kelsey, 2:220, where they are used for exactly the same purpose.

neque possessionem neque ius aliquod in provincias illas aut esse concessum aut potuisse concedi. Igitur aut inani tum titulo est affectus Carolus aut, si quid accepit, accepit illa quae in Italia extra Langobardicum regnum erant cum iuribus occupandi ea quae Constantinopolitanus imperator possidebat. Ceterum, cum quae Constantinopolitani possiderunt iure possiderint, in illa certe nihil iuris potuit Carolus nancisci. Sed nec in ea Carolus quidquam sibi sumpsit, eoque laboravit in fraternitatem et amicitiam assumi caesarum Constantinopolitanorum. Eam vero impetravit primum quidem a Nicephoro anno 820., testibus Annalibus Francicis et *Adone*, iterum ab eodem anno 810. redditis Venetiis, quod iidem testantur Annales, tertium a Michaele Nicephori successore anno 812., et ultimo a Leone anno 813. iisdem testibus. Non arbitror extare hodie foederum et pactorum illorum litteras. Nam quod Sigonius *libro 4.* de regno Italiae scribit, in primo illo foedere *nominatim expressum, ut Veneti inter utrumque imperium positi liberi atque immunes et ab utroque securi viverent,* id nescio an fide nitatur antiquorum eius saeculi monumentorum. Certe Annales illi memorant Venetias a Pipino captas, redditas Nicephoro. Id certius: ex eo foedere Calabriam et maritimas civitates Liburniae, Istriae, et Dalmatiae mansisse orientali imperio. Testatur enim Eginhartus, Carolum totam Italiam tenuisse *ab Augusta praetoria usque in Calabriam inferiorem, in quae Graecorum ac Beneventanorum constat esse confinia. Histriam quoque Liburniam et Dalmatiam, exceptis maritimis civitatibus, quae ob*

have put, Charlemagne into possession of those provinces, or given him any legal right to possess them. Either Charles was endowed with an empty title or, if the title meant anything at all, he was put into possession of those parts of Italy that lay outside the Lombard kingdom along with the right to occupy the possessions of the emperor of Constantinople.

[C.b.i. It did not apply to all of Italy or the eastern empire]

But since the emperors of Constantinople were in legitimate possession of whatever they did possess, Charles could certainly not have acquired any right to those areas. Indeed, rather than trying to occupy anything at all, he tried to be accepted into the brotherhood and friendship of the emperors of Constantinople. He first gained the friendship of Nicephorus in 820,[56] as witness the *Frankish Annals* and Ado,[57] renewed it with the same emperor in 810 after he had returned Venice, witness the same *Frankish Annals*, confirmed it for a third time with Michael, the successor of Nicephorus, in 812,[58] and for a last time with Leo in 813, again on the witness of the *Frankish Annals*.

I do not believe that any records of these treaties and pacts are extant today. To be sure, Carlo Sigonio, *The Kingdom of Italy*, book four,[59] writes that the first treaty "explicitly stated that the Venetians, situated between the two empires, were to live in freedom, immunity, and security from both," but I am not sure that this is founded on contemporary evidence. The *Frankish Annals* definitely say that Venice was captured by Pipin and returned to Nicephorus.[60] But regardless of any doubts about Venice, by the terms of that treaty Calabria and the cities on the coasts of Liburnia, Istria, and Dalmatia certainly remained under the control of the eastern empire. As Einhard points out, Charles held all of Italy "from Augusta Praetoria to Calabria Inferior, where there is the boundary between the Greeks and the Beneventans. He also held Istria, Liburnia, and Dalmatia except

---

[56] A misprint shared by the *New Discourse* and all versions of the *Exercitatio*. The correct year is 802. The *Frankish Annals* for 802 report that envoys of Charles departed for Constantinople in order to meet with Empress Irene and returned in 803 with letters from her successor Emperor Nicephorus I.

[57] Ado of Vienne, *Chronicon*, year 802. See "Ex Adonis archiepiscopi Viennensis Chronico," in *Scriptores*, ed. Georg Heinrich Pertz, Monumenta Germaniae Historica (Hannover: Hahn, 1829), 2:315–26. See also *PL* 123:23–138. Ado actually mentions Irene, not Nicephorus.

[58] The *Exercitatio* has 811 instead of 812.

[59] Carlo Sigonio, *Historiarum de regno Italiae libri viginti*, 2 vols. (Hanoviae: Typis Wechelianis apud haeredes C. Marnii, 1613), bk. 4, year 802.

[60] *Annales Regum Francorum*, year 810.

amicitiam et iunctum cum eo foedus Constantinopolitanum imperatorem habere permisit. Firmum autem amicitiae foedus inter utrumque imperatorem tandem coiisse testatur idem Eginhartus, *imperatores etiam Constantinopolitani,* inquiens, *Nicephorus, Michael, et Leo ultro amicitiam et societatem eius expetentes complures ad eum misere legatos, cum quibus tamen propter susceptum a se imperatoris nomen, et ob hoc eis quasi qui imperium eis eripere vellet valde suspectum, foedus firmissimum statuit, ut nulla inter partes cuiuslibet scandali remaneret occasio. Erat enim semper Romanis et Graecis Francorum suspecta potentia.* Quo facit illud quod in Annalibus habetur, legatos Michaelis Carolum dixisse *imperatorem et* βασιλέα. Ne in Italiam quidem omnem ergo ob titulum imperatoris ius fuit Carolo, tantum abest inde illi collatum ius in reliqua etiam orientalis imperii.

XXVII. Ceterum, si ne illa quidem Italiae hactenus imperatoribus possessa omnia accepit Carolus, aut titulum solum impetravit, aut vero potestatem aliquam in eas terras quae extra Langobardorum regnum erant in Italia, hactenus vero fuerant quasi in patrimonio pontificis. Posterius sane est verum. Erat enim iam ante quidem Carolus patricius Romanus, adeoque iam tum forte eo nomine habebat aliquid in ipsam urbem Romam iuris, ast per imperatoriam dignitatem longe plus consecutus est. Namque fuit quidem patricii nomen non nisi dignitatis titulus a Constantino Magno institutus, teste Zosimo *libro 2.,* qua de re plura *lege 12. codicis Iustinianei titulo 3. libro 3.* In Carolo tamen videtur hoc nomine

for the cities on the coast, which he conceded to the emperor of Constantinople because of their friendship and the treaty they had concluded."[61] Einhard also declares that both emperors eventually entered into a firm treaty of friendship: "Emperors Nicephorus, Michael, and Leo of Constantinople, seeking Charles's friendship and alliance, sent several legates to him on their own initiative, with whom he entered into a firm treaty, so that no occasion for scandal would linger between the parties, in spite of his acceptance of the imperial title and their considerable suspicion that he intended to deprive them of the empire. For the power of the Franks was always suspect to the Romans and the Greeks."[62] Hence, according to the *Frankish Annals*, Emperor Michael's legates called Charles "emperor and king."[63] It follows that the imperial title did not even give Charles the right to rule all of Italy, much less the rest of the eastern empire.

[C.b.ii. It did apply to Rome and the papacy]

XXVII. If the imperial title did not put Charles into possession of every region in Italy that had so far been in the possession of the eastern emperors, it must either have been entirely empty or given him some kind of power over Italian lands that lay outside the Lombard kingdom but had previously belonged to the patrimony of the pope, as it were. Such is indeed the case. Prior to the events in question Charles had already become *Patricius* of Rome. At that time he may thus already have had some kind of right to the city of Rome, although the imperial dignity certainly increased his rights considerably. The patriciate, after all, was merely a title of honor established by Constantine the Great, witness Zosimus, book two,[64] and for more details *Codex Iustinianus*, book twelve, title three, law three.[65] In Charles's case,

---

[61] Einhard, "Vita Karoli Magni," chap. 15, in *Quellen zur Karolingischen Reichsgeschichte. Erster Teil*, ed. and trans. Rau, 184. See also *PL* 97:25–62, here 39B–C. Cf. *Two Lives of Charlemagne*, trans. Lewis Thorpe (Harmondsworth: Penguin, 1969), 46–90.

[62] Einhard, "Vita Karoli Magni," chap. 16; 186.

[63] *Annales Regum Francorum*, year 812. Conring, echoing the *Annals*, uses the Greek βασιλεύς. See M. McCormick, "Basileus," in *Oxford Dictionary of Byzantium*, 1:264.

[64] Zosimus, *Historia nova*, 2nd ed. (Ienae: Krebsianis, 1713), bk. 2, chap. 40. See also Zosimus, *Historia nova*, ed. Ludovicus Mendelssohn (Leipzig: Teubner, 1887). Cf. Zosimus, *Historia nova: The Decline of Rome*, trans. James J. Buchanan and Harold T. Davis (San Antonio: Trinity University Press, 1967); or Zosimus, *New History*, trans. Ronald T. Ridley (Canberra: Australian Association for Byzantine Studies, 1982).

[65] *Corpus iuris civilis in quatuor partes distinctum*, ed. Dionysius Gothofredus, 2 vols. (Francofurti ad Moenum: Sumptibus Societatis, typis B. C. Wustii sen., 1688). See also *Codex Iustinianus*, ed. Paul Krüger, vol. 2 of *Corpus Iuris Civilis* (Berlin: Weidmann, 1877), 454–55. Cf. A. Kazhdan, "Patrikios," in *Oxford Dictionary of Byzantium*, 3:1600.

ipsa exarchalis potestas significata. Nam et vivo patre audiit quidem patricius, ut videre est in litteris Stephani papae apud Baronium *ad annum 775.* Ipse tamen annos sui patriciatus solet numerare ab eo quo devicit Desiderium, non autem 781., quod scribit Otto Frisingensis *libro 5. capitulo 28.*, et vero eo anno Romae exceptus est ritibus exarchorum aut patriciorum Romanorum, ut diserte scribit Anastasius in vita Hadriani. Ut vero non patricii iure, revera tamen iam ante impetratam imperatoriam dignitatem, Carolo in ipsam urbem Romam multum fuisse potestatis, vel ex iis liquet quae habentur in Annalibus Francicis *ad annum 769.: Romae Adriano defuncto, Leo pontificatum suscepit, et mox per legatos suos claves confessionis sancti Petri ac vexillum Romanae urbis cum aliis muneribus regi misit, rogavitque ut aliquem de suis optimatibus Romam mitteret, qui populum Romanum ad suam fidem atque subiectionem firmaret. Missus est ad hoc Engelbertus.* Recitat priora illa de missis clavibus et vexillo Baronius quoque, sed stomachabundus in novatores, qui inde ausi sint colligere aliquam Caroli in urbem potestatem. Ipse autem veterator illa de in fidem et subiectionem suscipiendis Romanis callide omittit, nihil aliud addens, quam missum Engelbertum ad donaria et Hunnici belli manubias offerendas. Constat vero et Carolum nondum imperatorem causam Leonis papae et coniuratorum agitasse anno 800., teste Anastasio et auctore Annalium.

however, the patriciate seems to have signified the power of the Exarch. For even while his father was still alive he was already referred to as *Patricius*, as can be seen in a letter of Pope Stephen in Baronio for the year 775,[66] and he himself used to count the years of his patriciate from the time when he defeated Desiderius in 774, not from 781, in spite of what Otto of Freising writes in book five, chapter twenty-eight,[67] and 774 happens to be precisely the same year when he was welcomed in Rome with the ceremonies appropriate for Exarchs or Roman Patricians, as Anastasius writes explicitly in his *Life of Hadrian*.[68]

At the same time, well before he obtained the imperial dignity, Charles also had great powers over the city of Rome that were not founded on his patriciate. This is evident from the *Frankish Annals* for 796: "After Hadrian had died in Rome Leo took over the papacy. He immediately sent his legates with the keys of the confession of St. Peter, the standard of the city of Rome, and other presents to King Charles and asked him to send one of his nobles to Rome in order to confirm the people of Rome in their faith and subjection. Accordingly Charlemagne dispatched Engelbert to Rome." Even Baronio quotes the first part about sending the keys and the standard in order to complain about the newfanglers who dared to use this as evidence that Charles had some power over the city of Rome.[69] But the old fox slyly omits the part about the faith and subjection which the Romans were supposed to give to Charles, adding only that Engelbert was sent to offer treasure and booty from the war against the Huns.[70] Yet it is certain that even before he became emperor Charles prosecuted the conspirators against Pope Leo in 800, witness Anastasius and the *Frankish Annals*.[71]

---

[66] Baronio, *Annales ecclesiastici*, year 755. 775 is a misprint shared by the *New Discourse* and all versions of the *Exercitatio*.

[67] Otto of Freising, *Chronica sive historia de duabus civitatibus. Chronik oder die Geschichte der zwei Staaten*, ed. Walther Lammers, trans. Adolf Schmidt (Darmstadt: Wissenschaftliche Buchgesellschaft, 1972). Cf. Otto of Freising, *The Two Cities: A Chronicle of Universal History to the Year 1146 A. D.*, ed. Austin P. Evans and Charles Knapp, trans. Charles Christopher Mierow (New York: Columbia University Press, 1928), 352.

[68] In a passage cited by Baronio, *Annales ecclesiastici*, year 774.

[69] Baronio, *Annales ecclesiastici*, year 796.

[70] There is an untranslatable pun in the Latin: since Baronio calls the "newfanglers" *novatores*, Conring calls Baronio a *veterator*, an "oldfangler." He implies, not only that Baronio is an old hand at what he is doing, but also that he is much more like the newfanglers about whom he complains than he would care to admit.

[71] *Annales Regum Francorum*, year 800.

XXVIII.[xiii] Quicquid vero sit de potestate quam patricius habuit Carolus, haud difficile est probatu, per imperatorium titulum illi collatum ius omne in urbem, pontificem, exarchatum Ravennae, et alia oppida quaedam extra Langobardici regni fines posita, quae fuerant caesarum usque ad sollemnem illam rebellionem, qua Gregorio II. papa superstites imperii Romani reliquiae a Leone Isauro et secutis Constantinopolitanis caesaribus defecerunt. Testatur id de urbe Roma ipse Bellarminus *libro 1. de translatione imperii Romani capitulo 4.* Liquet id ex adoratione qua *more antiquorum principum* recens coronatus augustus a Leone pontifice est adoratus. *Annales Francici 801.* Liquet ex sententia lata in eos qui Leonem papam male mulctaverant. *Iidem loco citato.* Liquet ex subsequente *ordinatione Romanae urbis et pontificis. Iidem loco citato.* Referendum eodem, quod apud Eginhartum in testamento Carolino metropolitanas inter urbes regni eius primo loco numerentur *Roma, Ravenna.* Haec potestas caesarum mansit per plurima saecula, donec tandem post fatalem regiae maiestatis casum in Henrico IV. per Gregorium VII. coepit novus ille papalis dominatus omnibus hactenus saeculis inauditus. Ex eo vero tempore prisca illa et vera Caesarea potestas in urbem, pontificem, et oppida quae ratione proventuum quorundam in patrimonio Petri, aut rectius papae, esse dicitur, tantum non est intermortua.

[xiii] The original has "XXIII".

XXVIII. Whatever the case may be with the power Charles had as *Patricius*, however, it is not difficult to prove that the imperial title gave him the right to exercise complete control over the city of Rome, the pope, the exarchate of Ravenna, and certain towns outside the borders of the Lombard kingdom that had belonged to the emperors of Constantinople, until the religious rebellion under Pope Gregory II during which the western remnants of the Roman empire defected from Emperor Leo the Isaurian and his successors. Bellarmine himself says so about the city of Rome in *The Transfer of the Roman Empire*, book one, chapter four.[72] The same conclusion follows from Pope Leo's ceremonious adoration of the newly crowned Augustus "in the manner of the ancient princes," as the *Frankish Annals* put it for 801.[73] Furthermore, there is the sentence Charlemagne imposed on those who had maltreated Pope Leo (same book and chapter). And there is the subsequent "Ordination of the City of Rome and its Bishops" (same book and chapter once again). In this context it may also be pointed out that Charlemagne's testament, as quoted by Einhard,[74] lists Rome and Ravenna first among the metropolitan cities of his kingdom.

This imperial power remained intact for several centuries until at last the royal majesty suffered a fatal collapse under Emperor Henry IV, and Pope Gregory VII inaugurated that new form of papal domination that had been unheard of in all the preceding centuries. Since that time the old and true power of the emperor over the city of Rome, the pope, and the towns that are for certain reasons said to belong the patrimony of Peter or, more correctly, the pope—that power has all but died away.

---

[72] Roberto Bellarmino, *De translatione imperii Romani a Graecis ad Francos, adversus Matthiam Flaccium Illyricum libri tres* (Antverpiae: Ex officina C. Plantini, 1589). In bk. 1, chap. 4, 87–108, Bellarmine listed thirty-one separately numbered (and a few more unnumbered) pieces of evidence, taken from authors ranging in chronological order from Zonaras to Albert Krantz, in order to prove that the pope transferred the Roman empire from the Greeks to the Franks by his sole authority. Conring was able to quote Bellarmine against himself because he granted freely that the pope played a central role in the events of Christmas 800, but reinterpreted his actions as those, not of the head of the western Church, but of a leading citizen of Rome; cf. Seifert, *Der Rückzug der biblischen Prophetie*, 174–75, 179–80, above, Introduction, n. 18.

[73] *Annales regum Francorum*, year 801. Bellarmine, in the just mentioned *De translatione imperii Romani*, bk. 1, chap. 4, 92–93, quoted the Frankish annals for 801 as the fifth item supporting his claims for papal authority. But he quoted them only so far as they did support those claims. He omitted the passage quoted by Conring. Conring was obviously delighted to have caught Bellarmine in subterfuge and to be able to turn a source invoked by Bellarmine himself against his purposes.

[74] Einhard, "Vita Karoli Magni," chap. 33.

XXIX. Quin itaque Carolus hanc solum potestatem titulo imperatoris sit consecutus, et quin haec pauca tantum magnifico illo augusti et imperatoris caesarisque nomine tum quidem venerint, neque aliud tum pertinuerit ad imperium Romanum occidentale, nihil sane est dubitandum. Videndum an sequentibus temporibus revera plus accesserit imperio illi Romano praeter ista pauca Italiae, et quidem an populo Romano eiusque caesaribus occidentalibus aliquid aut de novo fuerit partum, quod olim non habuerunt, aut eorum quae dudum deperdita diximus recuperatum.[xiv] Ceterum, si quid horum factum, aut vi occupatum oportuit, aut vero provinciae[xv] quaedam ultro sese Romanam in ditionem dederunt. Sane nec in Hispania, nec in Gallia illa quae ad Rhodanum usque a Pyrenaeis montibus tendit, nec in Pannonia, nec in Dacia, nec in Britannia tale quidquam contigit. Neque enim Hungaros, neque Francogallos, neque Hispanos et Gothos, neque Anglos ac Scotos, vel ultro vel vi coactos se et sua Romano imperio post Caroli Magni aetatem dedidisse ullibi legere est. Multo minus vero idipsum est factum a septentrionalibus populis Danis, Suecis, Moschis, Polonis, Lituanis, aliisque. Hinc vero sole est clarius, omnes has terras non tantum non pertinere hodie ad imperium Romanum, sed ne umbram quidem iuris Romano imperio in eas esse.

XXX. Fortassis tamen aliter se res habet de Italia Langobardica et Germania. Non sunt quidem illae terrae post Caroli aetatem a Romano populo victae, adeoque iure belli nunc non possidentur. Forte tamen sponte sua sese illis reliquiis antiquis sive subiecerunt, sive sociarunt in unum reipublicae corpus. Neque vero inanis forte illa suspicio est. Hodie enim receptum est illas terras omnes unius imperii Romani nomine nuncupare, quin obtinuit illud ipsum iam plus quam quingentos annos. Summus quoque magistratus populorum illorum per multa saecula non alio nomine quam imperatoris Romani audivit. Quod enim nunc adiicitur Germaniae regis titulus, id nuperum est inventum et vix ducentis annis auditum.

[xiv] 1674: "Videndum an sequentibus temporibus revera plus accesserit imperio illi Romano eiusque caesaribus occidentalibus aliquid, aut de novo fuerit partum quod olim non habuerunt, aut eorum quae dudum deperdita diximus recuperatum."

[xv] 1674: "aut vero regiones."

[D. Were Germany and Italy ever absorbed into the Roman empire?]

XXIX. There can then be no reasonable doubt that this was the sole extent of the power that Charles acquired with the imperial title; that the magnificent appellations "Augustus," "emperor," and "Caesar" applied only to a small part of Italy; and that nothing else belonged to the western Roman empire at that time. Now let us consider if anything else came under the control of the Roman empire thereafter, either because the people of Rome and its western emperors acquired something new they had not had in the past or because they recovered some of the losses we described above.[75] And if anything like that did happen, we also need to consider if it had to be done by force or if any provinces[76] surrendered to Roman rule of their own free will.

Certainly no such thing happened in Spain, in France from the Rhône to the Pyrenees, in Pannonia, in Dacia, or in Britain. For nowhere can we read that the Hungarians, the French, the Spaniards and Goths, or the Angles and Scots surrendered themselves and their own to the Roman empire after the age of Charlemagne, either voluntarily or compelled by force. Much less did the Danes, Swedes, Muscovites, Poles, Lithuanians, or any other people of the north do so. Hence it is clearer than the light of the sun, not only that these lands do not belong to the Roman empire today, but also that the Roman empire has not even a shadow of a right to them.

XXX. Things might be different with Lombard Italy and Germany, however. To be sure, the Roman people did not conquer those lands after the age of Charlemagne and therefore do not possess them now by right of war. But possibly Italy and Germany subjected themselves to those ancient remnants of the empire of their own free will, or joined with them to form a single state. Such a hypothesis is not altogether unfounded. It is common practice nowadays to refer to all of these lands simply as the Roman empire, as has indeed been done for more than five hundred years. Moreover, the highest magistrate of Germany and Italy has for several centuries been called no other name than Roman emperor, for the addition of the title "king of Germany" is a recent invention, barely two hundred years old.

---

[75] In the version of 1674 Conring consolidated this sentence as follows: "Now let us consider if anything else came under the control of the Roman empire and its western emperors thereafter, either because they gained something they had not had before or because they recovered some of the losses we described above."

[76] In the version of 1674 Conring substituted "regions" for "provinces."

XXXI. Verum enimvero, si quid tale umquam contigit, id aut ab ipso est Carolo Magno factum, aut ab eius successoribus. Carolum autem Magnum id egisse, falsissimum est. Certe non eo tempore id ille fecit, cum imperatorium titulum accepit. Non enim tale quid memorant annales et monumenta eius temporis, non tacitura certe rem tam magni momenti. Nec vero potuit id fieri. Neque enim licuit Carolo disponere quidquam de rebus regni Francici inconsultis ordinibus, quod alibi ostenditur. Tum autem temporis profecto non consuluerat Carolus ordines Francicos. Inopinato enim oblatus illi titulus est caesareus. Testatur enim Eginhartus dicere solitum Carolum, *se eo die, quamvis praecipue sollemniter esset, ecclesiam non intraturum fuisse, si pontificis consilium praescire potuisset.* Sed neque postea huiusmodi quid ab eo factum memorant ullae historiae veteres. Contra vero in diplomatibus eius et litteris cernere est distinctos titulos imperatoris et regni Francici ac Langobardici. Privilegium Osnabrugensis episcopatus apud Crancium *libro 1. metropolis, capitulo 2.* ita incipit: *Carolus imperator augustus Romanum gubernans imperium, dominus et rex Francorum et Langobardorum, Frisiorum dominator et Saxonum.* Datum autem illud est anno 805. Testamento quoque Carolino, quod Pithoeus edidit, et annalibus suis *ad annum 806.* inseruit Baronius, praefigitur *imperator caesar Carolus rex Francorum etc. Romani tutor imperii.* In alteris quoque eiusdem testamento, quo de mobilibus bonis disponitur apud Eginhartum, seorsim numerantur anni regni Franciae, regni Italiae, et imperii. Carolus itaque Italiam et Germaniam ab imperio numquam non distinxit.

[D.a. Germany, Italy, and the empire from Charlemagne to Otto the Great]

[D.a.i. Charlemagne]

XXXI. Now if any such thing did ever happen, it was done either by Charlemagne himself or by his successors. That Charlemagne did so is manifestly false. He certainly did not do so at the time when he accepted the imperial title. Contemporaneous annals and monuments record nothing of the kind, and they would surely not have been silent about a matter of such moment. Nor could he have done so, because he had no right to dispose over the affairs of the kingdom of the Franks without consulting the estates, as is shown elsewhere. Since Charles was not even aware that the imperial title would be conferred upon him, he had certainly not consulted the Frankish estates ahead of time. For Einhard points out that Charles used to say, "if he had known the pope's design, he would not have entered the church on that day, even though it was a great holiday."[77] Nor do the old histories record that he did anything like it later on. To the contrary, his charters and letters clearly distinguish between the titles of emperor, king of the Franks, and king of the Lombards. The privilege he granted to the bishop of Osnabrück, edited by Krantz, *Metropolis*, book one, chapter two,[78] begins like this: "Charles, emperor augustus, governing the Roman empire, lord and king of the Franks and Lombards, conqueror of the Frisians and Saxons." This dates from 805. Again, Charles's testament as edited by Pithou[79] and inserted in Baronio's *Annals* for 806 is inscribed: "Emperor Caesar Charles, king of the Franks etc., guardian of the Roman empire." And in other parts of the same testament, as reported by Einhard,[80] where dispositions are made about movable goods, the years of Charles's rule over the kingdom of France, the kingdom of Italy, and the empire are counted separately. Charles thus consistently distinguished Italy and Germany from the empire.

---

[77] Einhard, "Vita Karoli Magni," chap. 28.

[78] Albert Krantz, *Ecclesiastica historia, sive Metropolis*, rev. ed. (Francofurti ad Moenum: Ex officina typographica And. Wecheli, 1576).

[79] Pierre Pithou, *Annalium et historiae Francorum ab anno Christi DCCCCXC. scriptores coaetanei XII*, rev. ed. (Francofurti: Apud Andreae Wecheli heredes, Claudium Marnium, & Ioann. Aubrium, 1594), 283–88. Cf. Baronio, *Annales ecclesiastici*, year 806.

[80] Einhard, "Vita Karoli Magni," chap. 33.

XXXII. Sed et Ludovicus Pius Germaniam non minus atque Galliam, adeoque omnes certe regiones[xvi] transalpinas, ab imperii Romani reverentia voluit esse liberam.[xvii] Diviso enim inter tres filios regno suo, omnes pari voluit auctoritate esse, nequaquam autem aliqua in re Lothario, etsi ille caesareo honore esset insigniendus, inferior.[xviii] De ea divisione notatu digna sunt verba Trithemii in Annalibus Francicis. *Partitio talis est: regnum Francorum Germaniae perpetuo per se habeat proprium regem nulli penitus mortalium ne Romano quidem imperio subiectum, sed pristina Francorum consuetudine liberrimum. Regnum quoque Francorum Gallorum a nostro divisum simili modo regem, ut constitutio sonat, proprium habet liberum, qui non minus quam rex Germaniae liber sit et nulli omnino subiectus. Manifestum enim est, quod Franci ab origine semper fuerint liberrimi et neque Romanis, neque alteri alicui certe umquam servierint aut extiterint subiecti. Quin potius ipsi destruxerunt Romanorum imperium sibique fecere subiectum. Et propterea reges ambo in divisione regni pristinam libertatem Francorum ubique alter alteri illaesam servare statuerunt.* Porro nec Italiam Langobardicam alius ille conditionis fecit. Etsi enim illam una cum imperiali dignitate voluerit esse penes unum Lotharium, per accidens tamen ea tantum coniunxit, non autem quasi dederit Langobardicum regnum Romano imperio. Certe id factum nullibi legere est. Bene proinde Hugo Grotius *libro 2. de iure belli ac pacis capitulo 9. numero 11.: Carolus Magnus eiusque successores ius imperii quod habebant in Francos, ut et in Langobardos, a iure imperii in Romanos, ut nova ex causa quaesito, sollicite distinxerunt.*

XXXIII. Et vero sollicite haec observata fuerunt diu post Ludovicum. Cum enim Lotharius filius eius natu maximus propter primogeniturae et caesareae dignitatis honorem sibi ius aliquod in fratres arrogaret, orto inde bello victoque

---

[xvi] 1674: "omnes saltim regiones."

[xvii] 1674: "voluit esse liberas."

[xviii] 1674: "Diviso sane inter tres filios regno illius, omnes paris facti sunt auctoritatis, nequaquam autem aliquam in re Lothario, etsi ille caesareo honore esset insignitus, inferiores."

[D.a.ii. Louis the Pious]

XXXII. Louis the Pious also wanted both Germany and France, which is to say, all transalpine regions, to be free from having to pay reverence to the Roman empire. When he divided his kingdom among his three sons, he wanted each of them to have the same degree of authority, and none of them to be inferior to Lothar in any way,[81] even though Lothar was to be distinguished by the imperial honor. Regarding this division, it is worth quoting Trithemius on the *Frankish Annals*: "Here are the terms of the partition: the kingdom of the Franks of Germany shall always have its own king, who shall be subject to no human being, not even to the Roman empire, but completely free, as is the original custom of the Franks. And the kingdom of the Franks of Gaul, distinct from ours, shall similarly have its own free king, as the constitution says, who shall be no less free than the king of Germany and subject to no one at all. For it is manifest that from the very beginning the Franks have always been completely free and surely never served, or were subjected by, the Romans or anyone else. To the contrary, they destroyed the Roman empire and subjected it to themselves. When they divided the kingdom, both kings therefore decided that neither one of them would in any way infringe upon the original liberty of the Franks due to the other."[82] Furthermore, Louis made no other arrangements for Lombard Italy. He did want Lothar alone to hold Italy in conjunction with the imperial dignity, but the connection was purely coincidental and did not signify that the Lombard kingdom had been surrendered to the Roman empire. We can certainly find no information about any such surrender. Hugo Grotius, *The Law of War and Peace*, book two, chapter nine, number eleven, puts it well: "Charlemagne and his successors carefully distinguished their right of empire over the Franks and Lombards from their right of empire over the Romans, because the latter stemmed from a different source."

[D.a.iii. The later Carolingians]

XXXIII. Indeed, these distinctions were carefully observed long after Louis' reign. When his oldest son Lothar relied on primogeniture and the honor of the imperial dignity to claim a certain right over his brothers, a war broke out in

---

[81] In the version of 1674 Conring changed this from something of which Louis the Pious merely wished that it were so into something that was a matter of fact: "Each was given the same degree of authority, and no brother was inferior to Lothar in any way."

[82] This passage is compiled from two separate sections in Johannes Trithemius's dedicatory letter to the bishop of Würzburg preceding his *Compendium sive breviarium primi voluminis annalium sive historiarum de origine regum et gentis Francorum* (Parisiis: In officina Christiani Wecheli, sub scuto Basiliensi in vico Iacobaeo, 1539).

Lothario, libertatem suam fratres egregie tutati sunt. Ea de re in medio sunt verba Hincmari archiepiscopi Rhemensis, viri ea aetate summae auctoritatis, *epistola 1. capitulo 4. ad Ludovicum Balbum: qui cum Lothario erant immiserunt illum in hoc, ut fratres suos exheredaret et regni primores qui cum illis erant annullaret, quoniam ipse primogenitus et nomine imperatoris erat. Illi autem qui erant cum Carolo et Ludovico dicebant, quod seniores illorum* (id est, domini sui Carolus et Ludovicus) *Lotharii fratres erant, et sacramento regnum inter illos divisum fuerat, et illi nec genere nec potestate inferiores erant, et ideo non se contra illos concederent.* Latius omnia ista narrat Nithardus libro 4., ubi inter alia post fatalem illam inter tres fratres pugnam scribit missos a Lothario legatos ad Carolum et Ludovicum, qui nomine Lotharii dicerent, *si vellent illi aliquid illi supra tertiam partem*[xix] *regni propter nomen imperatoris, quod illi pater illorum concesserat, et propter dignitatem imperii, quam avus regno Francorum adiecerat, facerent. Sin aliter, tertiam tantummodo partem totius sibi concederent, regeretque quisque illorum portionem regni sui prout melius posset, frueretur alter alterius subsidio et benevolentia.* Et vero posterius placuit. Itaque Ludovico cessit Germania pleno iure et nulla in re dependens ab imperio Romano gubernanda non minus atque Gallia Carolo. Non latuerunt haec Baronium. Itaque *ad annum 848.* Trithemium his verbis accusat: *errat dum ait iussu Lotharii convenisse* (Germaniae episcopi[xx]), *cum id factum per Ludovicum regem esse in regno ipsius non sit dubium, nam nullam Lotharium facultatem habuisse disponendi aliquid in regno Germaniae spectante ad Ludovicum certum est.*

[xix] The grammar would seem to require something like "aliquid illi concedere supra tertiam partem."

[xx] "episcopus" in the original.

which Lothar was defeated while his brothers preserved their liberty splendidly. Here the words of Archbishop Hincmar of Rheims, who enjoyed extraordinary authority at that time, in his first letter to Louis the Stammerer,[83] chapter four, are directly relevant: "Lothar's followers incited him to disinherit his brothers and to destroy the nobles of the kingdom supporting them, because he was the firstborn and had the imperial title. But the supporters of Charles and Louis said that their seniors (that is, their lords Charles and Louis) were Lothar's brothers, that the kingdom had been divided among them by a sworn agreement, and that they were inferior neither by descent nor by power. And thus they refused to change sides against the will of their lords."[84] Nithard, book four, talks about all of this at greater length, where he writes among other things that after the decisive battle among the three brothers Lothar sent legates to Charles and Louis, who said the following on his behalf: "If Charles and Louis, out of respect for the imperial title that their father had bestowed on him, and the dignity of the empire that their grandfather had added to the kingdom of the Franks, were willing to give him more than a third of the kingdom, they should do so; if not, they should leave him just a third of the whole, and each of them should rule his part of the kingdom as he saw fit and enjoy the others' aid and good will."[85] And the second alternative was the one that was accepted. Hence Germany came under Louis' exclusive jurisdiction and was to be governed without any dependence on the Roman empire, while France came under Charles's jurisdiction in the same way. Baronio is fully aware of this, for under the year 848 he criticizes Trithemius as follows: "He is mistaken when he says that they (the bishops of Germany)[86] assembled on Lothar's orders. There is no doubt that this happened on King Louis' orders in King Louis' kingdom, for Lothar surely had no right to dispose over anything in the kingdom of Germany, since that belonged to Louis."[87]

---

[83] Louis III, ruled Germany from 876 to 882.

[84] Hincmar of Reims, "Ad Ludovicum Balbum regem: Novi regis instructio ad rectam regni administrationem," in *Hincmari archiepiscopi Remensis opera duos in tomos digesta*, ed. Jacques Sirmond, 2 vols. (Lutetiae Parisiorum: Sumtibus Sebastiani Cramoisy, 1645), 2:179–84. See also *PL* 125:983–990. The document dates to 877, but refers back to the war between the sons of Louis the Pious in the early 840s.

[85] Nithard, "Historiarum libri IIII," bk. 4, chap. 3, in *Quellen zur Karolingischen Reichsgeschichte. Erster Teil*, ed. and trans. Rau, 385–461, here 450. See also *PL* 116:45–76, here 72B–C. Cf. *Carolingian Chronicles: Royal Frankish Annals and Nithard's Histories*, trans. Scholz, 127–74, here 168.

[86] The original has "the bishop of Germany."

[87] Baronio, *Annales ecclesiastici*, year 848, referring to Johannes Trithemius, *Chronicon insigne monasterii Hirsaugiensis* (Basileae: Apud Iacobum Parcum, 1559), year 848, on the synod of Mainz—another example of quoting an author in spite of himself.

XXXIV. Mansisse eandem libertatem Germanici regni, superstite Carolina regum familia, certum est. Plerique enim qui illi praefuerunt cum Italia aut cum imperio nihil habuerunt commercii. Diviso enim post obitum Ludovici Germanici regno, Carolus et Ludovicus et Carolomannus singuli suam regni partem propria auctoritate tenuerunt, ut constat ex *historia landgraviorum Thuringiae capitulo 6*. Arnolphus quoque diu Germaniam rexit anteaquam imperatoriam dignitatem consequeretur. Post hunc vero neque Ludovicus neque Conradus vel Italiam vel imperium habuit. Quo satis constat ea certe tempestate Germaniam non fuisse partem imperii, nec administratam fuisse auctoritate caesarea, sed proprios sibi reges habuisse, et liberam fuisse distinctamque et sui iuris rempublicam.

XXXV. Italiae quidem regnum qui tenuere, iidem fere et imperatores fuerunt. Immo ea occasione post obitum Caroli Crassi in Italia pontifices deliberarunt de eligendo imposterum aliquo Italiae rege cum imperatorio titulo, quod testatur Carolus Sigonius *libro 5. de regno Italiae*. Fuere tamen et reges Italiae sine titulo imperatorio. Nec interea temporis constat factum aliquod decretum consensu Carolinae familiae (penes quam ius erat hereditarium in regnum Langobardicum) de subiiciendo illo regno imperii Romani auctoritati et legibus. Itaque et Langobardicum regnum eo tempore mansit liberum ab imperii Romani potestate.

XXXVI. Extincta porro Carolina familia, Henricus Auceps eiusque filius Otto Magnus ab anno 919. ad 962. Germaniae regnum cum regno Lotharii tenuerunt, nulla caesarea dignitate ornati, nullo etiam modo imperium aliquod Romanum reverentes. Neque enim verum est, quod nonnulli evincere pertendunt, Henricum Aucupem fuisse caesarem. Quin alibi ostenditur, illum ne quidem

XXXIV. We know that this liberty of the German kingdom remained intact as long as the Carolingian royal family survived. Most of the kings who presided over Germany at that time had no dealings with Italy or the empire at all. When Louis the German died and the kingdom was divided among his sons Charles, Louis, and Carloman, each ruled his part of the kingdom by his own authority, as is apparent from the *History of the Landgraves of Thuringia*, chapter six.[88] Arnulf likewise ruled Germany for a long time before he acquired the imperial dignity. Thereafter neither Louis nor Conrad controlled either Italy or the empire. This is enough to prove that at least at that time Germany was neither included in the empire nor administered by imperial authority, but had its own kings and was a free, independent, and autonomous state.

XXXV. The kings who ruled Italy, on the other hand, usually became emperors as well. This is why after the death of Charles the Fat the bishops of Italy[89] considered the possibility that they might henceforth elect a king of Italy and confer the imperial title on him at the same time, as testifies Carlo Sigonio, *The Kingdom of Italy*, book five.[90] But there were also kings of Italy who did not have the imperial title. Meanwhile the Carolingian family, which enjoyed hereditary rights over the Lombard kingdom, is not known to have consented to any decree subjecting Lombardy to the authority and laws of the Roman empire. It follows that at that time the Lombard kingdom, too, continued to be free from the power of the Roman empire.

[D.a.iv. Henry the Fowler and Otto the Great]

XXXVI. When the Carolingian family had died out, Henry the Fowler and his son Otto the Great ruled the kingdom of Germany and the kingdom of Lothar from 919 to 962 without having been decorated with the imperial dignity, and without paying reverence to the Roman empire in any way. For it is not true, as some pretend to prove,[91] that Henry the Fowler was emperor. To the contrary, as is shown

---

[88] "Historia Erphesfordensis anonymi scriptoris de landgraviis Thuringiae," in *Illustrium veterum scriptorum, qui rerum a Germanis per multas aetates gestarum historias vel annales posteris reliquerunt, tomus unus*, ed. Johannes Pistorius, 2 vols. (Francofurti: Impensis C. Marnii haeredum, I. & A. Marnii, 1583), 1:908–60.

[89] "After the death of Charles the Fat in Italy, the bishops considered the possibility . . ." would be a more natural way to translate the Latin. But Charles the Fat died in Swabia, not in Italy.

[90] Carlo Sigonio, *Historiarum de regno Italiae libri viginti*, bk. 5, year 884 (p. 138 in the edition Hanoviae: Typis Wechelianis, 1613).

[91] I am not sure to whom Conring is referring here.

iura habuisse ad occupandam Italiam aut imperii dignitatem postulandam. Sane nihil Italiae illum possedisse est certum. Etiam illa ergo aetate Germania non fuit habita imperii Romani portio. Eodem vero tempore nunc Berengarius dux Foroiuliensis, mox Lambertus, iterum Ludovicus Burgundus, modo Rudolphus Burgundus, modo Hugo Arelatensis, eiusque filius Lotharius, nec non denique Berengarius Eporegiae marchio ab Italiae optimatibus, inconsulto vel populo vel pontifice Romano, immo his nihil contra nitentibus, Italiae reges sunt creati Papiae, regni Langobardici metropolitana urbe. Et vero horum vix unus alterque caesareum titulum accepit. Quo iterum constat, etiam tum temporis et Langobardicum regnum fuisse liberam rempublicam, reliquias vero illas imperii Romani ab hoc regno seiunctas fuisse, et plerumque sub nullo imperatore.

XXXVII. Otto quoque Magnus non Germaniam tantum, sed et Italicum illud Langobardorum regnum diu habuit in potestate sua, ante quam imperator Romanus audiret. Namque anno 951. invitatus ab Adelheide vidua Lotharii regis, quam et mox in matrimonium duxit, fudit omnique potestate exuit Berengarium regem Italiae eiusque filium Adelbertum. Witikindus Corbeiensis *libro 3.* scribit, Ottonem *cum Adelheide Papiam, quae est sedes regia, obtinuisse.* Sequenti anno 952. Berengarius et Adelbertus in gratiam recepti feudi iure ab Ottone regnum Langobardicum recuperarunt. Illam rem ita narrat continuator Reginonis: *Berengarius cum filio Adelberto sese subiiciens Ottoni ab eo ut subditus recipit regendam Italiam.* Iisdem verbis utitur ipse Baronius *tomo 10. annalium ad annum 952.* Witikindus ita loquitur: *cum conventus fieret, Berengarius manus filii sui Adelberti suis manibus implicans renovata fide coram omni exercitu famulatui regis se cum filio suo subiugavit, et ita dimissus in Italiam remeavit cum gratia et pace.*

elsewhere, he did not even have the right to occupy Italy or to ask for the imperial dignity. It is in fact certain that he possessed no part of Italy at all. Even at that time, therefore, Germany was still not considered to be part of the Roman empire.

During the same period the nobles of Italy made Duke Berengar of Friuli, Lambert, Louis of Burgundy, Rudolph of Burgundy, Hugh of Arles, his son Lothar, and finally Margrave Berengar of Ivrea one after the other kings of Italy in Pavia, the capital of the Lombard kingdom, without consulting the people or bishop of Rome and even without any Roman opposition. But barely one or two of these kings accepted the imperial title. That proves once again that the Lombard kingdom, too, was still an independent state, that the remnants of the Roman empire were separated from Lombardy, and that most of the time they were subject to no emperor at all.

XXXVII. Otto the Great himself ruled not only Germany but also the Lombard kingdom in Italy long before he was called Roman emperor. In 951, when Adelheid, King Lothar's widow, whom he was going to marry soon thereafter, invited him to Italy, he routed King Berengar of Italy and his son Adelbert and deprived them of their power. Widukind of Corvey, book three, writes that Otto "obtained Pavia, the royal seat, together with Adelheid."[92] In the following year 952, Berengar and Adelbert were received into Otto's good graces and recovered the Lombard kingdom from him by feudal law. The continuator of Regino puts this event in the following words: "Berengar and his son Adelbert submitted to Otto in order to be able to rule Italy as his subjects."[93] Baronio himself uses the same words in volume ten of his *Annals* for the year 952.[94] And Widukind writes: "During the assembly Berengar folded the hands of his son Adelbert in his own, renewed his faith in front of the entire army, and subjected himself and his son to the king's servitude. On those terms he was dismissed and returned to Italy in grace and peace."[95]

---

[92] Widukind, "Res gestae Saxonicae," bk. 3, chap. 9, in *Quellen zur Geschichte der Sächsischen Kaiserzeit*, ed. and trans. Albert Bauer and Reinhold Rau (Darmstadt: Wissenschaftliche Buchgesellschaft, 1977), 1–183, here 134. See also *PL* 137:123–212. Cf. Widukind, *The Three Books of the Deeds of the Saxons*, trans. Raymund F. Wood (Ph.D. Diss., University of California, Los Angeles, 1949).

[93] Adalbert, "Continuatio Reginonis," year 952, in *Quellen zur Geschichte der Sächsischen Kaiserzeit*, ed. and trans. Bauer and Rau, 185–231, here 206. See also *PL* 132:151–174, here 162B.

[94] Volume 16 in the edition Lucae: Typis L. Venturini, 1738–1759.

[95] Widukind, "Res gestae Saxonicae," bk. 3, chap. 11.

XXXVIII. Itaque iam tum feudi iure ab Ottone Langobardicum regnum obtinuit Berengarius. Et tamen anno demum 961. Otto, a multis Langobardici regni proceribus et Ioanne papa contra Berengarii tyrannidem invitatus, expulso Berengario et liberato papa, primo quidem regnum Italiae occupavit iterum, deinde anno sequente imperator est creatus. Narrat Baronius *ad annum 961.* ex historia ducum Beneventinorum antiqua, proceres Italiae, appropinquante iam Ottone, Adelberto filio Berengarii regis dixisse: *vellemus domine, ut Papiam cum paucis pergas et tuo genitori dicas, quatenus Langobardorum regnum sub vestra ditione committat, quia nos minime sub illius potestate amplius iam durabimus. Si vobis committit regnum, nos totis viribus pugnabimus, sin autem non, Italiae regnum extero regi committemus.* Idipsum autem cum Adelbertus non potuisset impetrare, proceres omnes Berengarium pariter et Adelbertum reliquisse. Addit autem ille scriptor: *itaque Otto rex sine impedimento in Italiam introivit atque Italiae regnum obtinuit.* Luitprandus, qui itidem eo tempore vixit, in narratione legationis suae Constantinopolitanae, quam a Canisio editam inseruit Baronius decimo annalium tomo *ad annum 968.*, ita rem omnem narrat Nicephoro imperatori: *palam est quod Berengarius et Adelbertus, sui milites* (id est, Ottonis vasalli) *effecti, regnum Italicum sceptro aureo ex eius manu susceperunt, et praesentibus servis tuis qui nunc usque supersunt iureiurando fidem promiserunt. Et quia hanc perfide violarunt, iuste illos quasi desertores sibique rebelles regno privavit.* Tenuit ergo etiam Otto Langobardicum regnum antequam caesarea iura esset consecutus, adeoque et regnum illud Italiae cum imperii iuribus nihil habuit commercii. Etsi vero sequente anno Otto imperator sit creatus, etiam tum tamen satis curate distinxit Italicum illud regnum a

XXXVIII. Already at that time Berengar thus obtained the Lombard kingdom from Otto by feudal law. Eventually, however, in 961 many nobles of the Lombard kingdom and Pope John invited Otto to overthrow the tyranny of Berengar. He expelled Berengar, liberated the pope, occupied the kingdom of Italy once again, and became emperor in the following year. Baronio, drawing on the old history of the dukes of Benevento,[96] reports for the year 961 that, when Otto was already approaching, the nobles of Italy announced to Adelbert, son of King Berengar: "We ask you, Lord, that you march with a few men to Pavia and tell your father to commit the kingdom of the Lombards to your rule, because we refuse to remain under his power any longer. If he does commit the kingdom to you, we shall defend it with all our might, but if not, we shall commit it to a king from elsewhere." And when Adelbert failed to obtain the kingdom from his father, all of the nobles did in fact abandon them both. The writer adds: "Thus King Otto entered Italy without any obstacles and seized control over the kingdom of Italy."

In the report of his legation to Constantinople, which has been edited by Canisius[97] and incorporated by Baronio in his *Annals*, volume ten,[98] for the year 968, Liudprand, who lived at the same time, described the entire affair in the following terms to Emperor Nicephorus: "It is obvious that Berengar and Adelbert became his knights (that is, vassals of Otto), received the kingdom of Italy by a golden sceptre from his hand, and swore an oath of fealty in the presence of servants of yours who are still alive. And since they violated their oaths, Otto was right to deprive them of the kingdom as deserters and rebels against himself."[99]

Otto thus held the Lombard kingdom before he acquired imperial rights. It follows that the kingdom of Italy had nothing in common with the empire. And even though Otto became emperor the following year, he carefully distinguished

---

[96] The "old history of the dukes of Benevento" is the so-called *Chronicon Salernitanum*, ed. Ulla Westerbergh, Acta Universitatis Stockholmiensis, Studia Latina Stockholmiensia 3 (Stockholm: Almqvist & Wiksell, 1956), here chap. 169. See also "Chronicon Salernitanum," in *Scriptores*, ed. G. H. Pertz, Monumenta Germaniae Historica (Hannover: Hahn, 1839), 3:470–559.

[97] Henricus Canisius, ed., *Chronicon Victoris episcopi Tunnunensis. Chronicon Joannis Biclarensis... Legatio Luitprandi episcopi Cremonensis ad Nicephorum Phocam* (Ingolstadii: Officina typographica Ederiana, apud Andream Angermarium, 1600).

[98] Volume 16:176–91, in the edition I used.

[99] Liudprand of Cremona, "Legatio ad imperatorem Constantinopolitanum Nicephorum Phocam," in *Quellen zur Geschichte der Sächsischen Kaiserzeit*, ed. and trans. Bauer and Rau, 524–89, here chap. 5. See also *PL* 136:909–938. Cf. *The Works of Liudprand of Cremona*, trans. F. A. Wright (New York: E. P. Dutton, 1930), 233–77, and M. McCormick, "Liutprand of Cremona," in *Oxford Dictionary of Byzantium*, 2:1241–42, with bibliography.

reliquiis illis imperii Romani quas papa possidebat. Recitat Gratianus *capitulo 33. distinctione 63.* iuramentum Ottonis papae Ioanni praestitum, quod et Baronius habet *anno 960.*,[xxi] de cuius fide non est meum nunc disputare. Ibi diserte vero legitur: *cuicumque regnum Italicum commisero, iurare faciam illum, ut adiutor tui sit.* Habet idem Baronius *anno 962.* diploma, quo Otto creditur confirmasse Romanae ecclesiae bona, ubi inter alia legitur: *insuper offerimus tibi de proprio nostro regno civitates et oppida cum piscariis suis Reatem, Amiternum, etc.* Unde patet porro Ottonem Langobardicum regnum sibi arrogasse iure proprietario.

XXXIX. Insecutis temporibus aeterno quidem foedere iuncta est caesarea dignitas non minus atque Italici regni possessio cum Germania (quod quibus auctoribus, quave ratione, aut qua de causa contigerit, non est instituti nostri nunc exponere). Coepit etiam ex eo communis appellatio illa imperii Romani, quae res multos in errorem perduxit. Nullum tamen monumentum potest produci, nullae tabulae exstant, quibus possit probari, aut coiisse Germanicum et Italicum regnum cum illis imperii Romani reliquis in unam prorsus rempublicam, aut illa in imperii istius ditionem concessisse. Alterutrum autem affirmare sine certis documentis non licet aut fas est.

XL. Ac prius quidem vel illo uno potest abunde refelli, quod et Germania et Langobardicum regnum comitia sua de rebus maximis ad rempublicam pertinentibus omni tempore instituerit, egerit quoque res maximas non impetrato consensu vel papae vel aliorum imperii istius civium. Ingessit se quidem, fateor, papa Romanus post tempora Henrici IV. plerisque imperii negotiis, quin et conatus est pleraque ad arbitrium suum trahere. Numquam tamen ipse voluit videri deliberationibus interesse ut civis aliquis reipublicae, numquam etiam hoc nomine

---

[xxi] 1674: "966."

the Italian kingdom from the remnants of the Roman empire that were in the possession of the pope. Gratian quotes the oath sworn by Otto to Pope John in distinction sixty-three, chapter thirty-three,[100] and Baronio has it for the year 960.[101] I am not now going to discuss its trustworthiness.[102] But it does say there expressly that "to whomever I shall commit the kingdom of Italy, I will make him swear an oath that he will assist you." For 962 Baronio also quotes the charter in which Otto is believed to have confirmed the goods of the Roman Church, where one can read among other things that "we also endow you from our own kingdom with the cities and towns of Rieti, Amiterno, etc. with their fisheries." Whence it is evident once again that Otto claimed the Lombard kingdom by right of ownership.[103]

[D.b. Otto the Great's reorganization of the empire]

XXXIX. From that time on the imperial dignity and the Italian kingdom were joined by an everlasting bond to Germany. It is no part of our present purpose to explain the authors of, the reasons for, or the causes behind this event. But as a result it became common practice to refer to Germany as the Roman empire. This has misled a great many people. Nonetheless there are no monuments or tablets to prove either that the kingdoms of Germany and Italy formed a single state with the remnants of the Roman empire, or that they submitted to the rule of the empire—and to maintain either one of these assertions without supporting documents is neither permissible nor right.

[D.b.i. The assemblies of Germany and Italy]

XL. To the contrary, these assertions can be abundantly rebutted merely by pointing out that the kingdoms of Germany and Lombardy always held their own assemblies to deal with important affairs of state, and that they managed their affairs without asking for the consent of the pope or any other citizen of the empire. To be sure, after the times of Henry IV the Roman pope interfered in most affairs of the empire and even tried to subject them to his own decision. But he never wanted to be seen to participate in their deliberations as citizen of

---

[100] Gratian, *Decretum*, ed. E. Friedberg, vol. 1 of *Corpus Iuris Canonici* (Leipzig: B. Tauchnitz, 1879), col. 246.

[101] The version of 1674 has "966."

[102] He was going to do so in considerable detail in the *De Germanorum imperio Romano*, chap. 10, in *Opera*, 1:73–86.

[103] *Iure proprietario* in the Latin.

vel vocatus fuit vel admissus, sed quomodo in omnia alia regna et omnes orbis Christiani respublicas summa impietate dominatum sibi arrogavit et sumpsit, tamquam supremus monarcha a deo constitutus, ita et hoc nomine reipublicae Germanicae negotia voluit gubernare, saepe invitis, nonnumquam et consentientibus regni ordinibus fatali tum errore constrictis. Si Germanico vero regno et Italico mansit summum ius administrandi rempublicam suam sine populi Romani consensu, non in unam profecto rempublicam haec coierunt. Quot enim sunt summae potestates, totidem sunt respublicae, utut unum habeant principem, aut arcto aliquo foedere συμμαχίας civitates illae sint unitae. Quale quid de civitatibus Helveticis Iosias Simlerus et Bodinus, de foederatis Belgicogermanicis provinciis optime Hugo Grotius *in apologetico suo capitulo 1.* annotarunt. Ceterum non convenisse omnia illa in unam rempublicam, manifestum fit etiam diversis illis coronationibus regum nostrorum. Corona enim indicium est et signum quodammodo reipublicae. Seorsim vero primo accipitur corona regni Germanici, ex antiqua quidem consuetudine ut et lege Carolina, Aquisgrani.[xxii] Perperam enim vulgo creditur et nuncupatur[xxiii] illa corona caesarea. Veteres sane rectius (inter quos est et Fridericus I. caesar *epistola ad Ottonem Frisingensem*) dixere illam coronam

---

[xxii] 1674: "lege Carolina, quod nonnullis etsi falso placet, Aquisgrani."
[xxiii] "nuncupaturi" in the original.

any state, nor was he ever asked or allowed to participate in such deliberations on grounds of citizenship. He rather wanted to govern the affairs of Germany by the same title by which he usurped lordship over all other kingdoms and republics of the Christian world with such utter shamelessness: as supreme monarch established by God. Often he did so against the will of the estates of the kingdom, but sometimes he did so with their consent because they were entangled in a disastrous error at the time. But since the kingdoms of Germany and Italy retained the sovereign right to administer their states without the consent of the Roman people, they certainly did not form a single state with them. For there are as many states as there are sovereign powers, regardless of whether they are ruled by a single prince or consist of cities united by a treaty of confederation[104]—a point made about the Swiss cities by Josias Simmler[105] and Bodin,[106] and especially well about the united Belgian-German provinces by Hugo Grotius in his *Apologeticus*, chapter one.[107]

[D.b.ii. The German, Italian, and imperial crowns]

The different stages in the coronations of our kings furnish another proof that these kingdoms did not form a single state. For the crown is a kind of sign or symbol of the state. But according to ancient custom and a Carolingian law[108] the crown of the kingdom of Germany is accepted first, separately from the imperial crown, in Aix-la-Chapelle. The widespread belief that this is the imperial crown and the habit of referring to it accordingly are utterly wrong. The ancients, including Emperor Frederick I in a letter to Otto of Freising,[109] called it more correctly

---

[104] Conring uses the Greek συμμαχία.

[105] Josias Simmler, *De republica Helvetiorum libri duo* (Tiguri: Christophorus Froschoverus, 1576), passim.

[106] Jean Bodin, *Les six livres de la république*, ed. Christiane Fremont, Marie-Dominique Couzinet, and Henri Rochais, 6 vols. (Paris: Fayard, 1986), here bk. 1, chap. 7; 1:159–60, 165–67. Cf. Jean Bodin, *The Six Books of a Commonweale*, trans. Richard Knolles, ed. Kenneth D. McRae (Cambridge, MA: Harvard University Press, 1962).

[107] Hugo Grotius, *Apologeticus eorum qui Hollandiae Westfrisiaeque et vicinis quibusdam nationibus ex legibus praefuerunt ante mutationem quae evenit anno MDCXVIII.* (Parisiis: Sumptibus Nicolai Buon, 1622).

[108] In the version of 1674 Conring added: "which some, however, consider to be a forgery." I am not sure whom Conring had in mind.

[109] This is the letter placed at the beginning of Otto of Freising and Rahewin, *Gesta Frederici seu rectius Cronica*, ed. Franz-Josef Schmale, trans. Adolf Schmidt (Darmstadt: Wissenschaftliche Buchgesellschaft, 1965), 82–89, here 82. Cf. Otto of Freising and Rahewin, *The Deeds of Frederick Barbarossa*, trans. Charles Christopher Mierow and Richard Emery (New York: Columbia University Press, 1953), 17–20.

regni Teutonici. At caesaream coronam semper, et quidem iam per annos octingentos, solus papa Romanus addidit. Quin et multi post Ottonem papae[xxiv] quoque coronati sunt reges Langobardorum, adeoque triplici corona, Germaniae nempe, Langobardiae, et imperii Romani insigniti. Accedit, quod numquam quisquam post Carolum Magnum caesareum voluerit titulum usurpare ante acceptam coronam illam Romanam, etsi iam esset corona Germanici regni honoratus. Omnes enim ante sunt tantum reges dicti, etiam nunc non nisi electi caesares audiunt, licet coronati sint Germaniae aut Italiae reges. Ad hoc satis hodieque distinguunt ipsi caesares regnum Germanicum ab imperio Romano, dum electos se dicunt imperatores Romanos, sed addito titulo regum Germaniae, quod nempe aliud sit esse regem Germaniae, aliud electum caesarem Romani imperii.

XLI. Igitur unam profecto cum imperio Romano rempublicam neque Germania hodie neque Langobardicum regnum constituit. Tantum vero abest, Germaniam sese et Langobardiam a sese domitam Romano imperio subiecisse, ut contra potius illud olim Germaniae sese dederit magna ex parte. Omnem enim imperatores eligendi potestatem Romani eorumque pontifices in Germanos aeterna lege contulerunt, quo ipso ius Germanis dederunt summum magistratum Romano imperio creandi, quod est magnam maiestatis partem alteri tribuere, sibi eripere. Id quando ceperit, alias exponitur. Id certum vero est, moderatis adhuc paparum rebus, et ante monstrum illud hominis Hildebrandum[xxv] aut Gregorium VII. papam, magnam satis fuisse caesarum a Germanis electorum in pontificem et populum Romanum auctoritatem ac potentiam, et nihilominus tamen in Germanorum fuisse potestate eam omnem dignitatem ac vim electis ex suo arbitrio regibus suis in alienam rempublicam conferre. Quin manet hodieque, ut non nisi Germanorum rex audiat caesar, prisca auctoritate licet adempta. Quo patet, quasi surrogasse sibi potius Romanum populum in sua iura Germaniam, quam ut Germania sese illi imperio subiecerit.

[xxiv] 1674: "Papiae" is obviously correct.
[xxv] 1674: "monstrum illud ambitionis Hildebrandum."

the crown of the Teutonic kingdom. The imperial crown, on the other hand, has for more than eight hundred years always been bestowed by the Roman pope alone. After Otto the Great many kings were also crowned kings of Lombardy in Pavia,[110] so that they were distinguished by a triple crown, namely of Germany, Lombardy, and the Roman empire. One may add that after Charlemagne no one ever wished to claim the Roman imperial title until after he had been crowned with the Roman crown, even if he had already been honored with the crown of the German kingdom. For until that moment all of them were only called kings, and even nowadays they are only considered to be emperors-elect, even though they are crowned kings of Germany or Italy. In this respect the emperors continue even nowadays to distinguish rather clearly between the German kingdom and the Roman empire, calling themselves Roman emperors-elect while adding the title king of Germany, for it is assuredly one thing to be king of Germany and quite another to be emperor-elect of the Roman empire.

[D.b.iii. The election of the emperor]

XLI. Hence neither Germany nor the Lombard kingdom constitute a single state with the Roman empire today. Indeed, so far from Germany and German-ruled Lombardy having subjected themselves to the Roman empire, quite to the contrary, the Roman empire surrendered itself in great part to Germany. For the Romans and their bishops conferred the power to elect the emperor in its entirety by an eternal law to the Germans. It follows that they gave the Germans the right to appoint the highest magistrate of the Roman empire, which means that they attributed a substantial part of their sovereignty[111] to someone else and removed it from themselves. When this happened is explained elsewhere. But it is certain that as long as some restraints were still placed upon the conduct of the papacy, and before the reign of that monster of a man[112] Hildebrand, otherwise known as Pope Gregory VII, the emperors elected by the Germans enjoyed a considerable degree of authority and power over the bishop and people of Rome, and that it was even entirely within the power of the Germans and their freely elected kings to confer the imperial dignity and the power of electing the emperor upon some other state. Hence it is even nowadays still the case that no one is called emperor except the king of the Germans, even if he has long since been deprived of his ancient authority. Which proves that the Roman people turned their rights over to Germany, rather than that Germany subjected itself to their empire.

---

[110] The Latin has *papae* (pope), which makes no sense, except that it may perhaps be taken as a nice Freudian slip of the typographer.

[111] *Maiestas* in the Latin.

[112] In the version of 1674 Conring changed this into "monster of ambition."

XLII. Haec vero omnia cum longe sint certissima, nihil est, cur non aperte tandem pronunciemus, *neque Germaniam neque Langobardicum Italiae regnum vere partes esse Romani imperii, sed respublicas ab illo distinctas, adeoque nec imperatorem, in quantum est imperator, esse vel Germanici vel Langobardici regni caput aut magistratum, sed quatenus idem simul rex est.* Nec vero ex eo, quod iam multis saeculis vulgo Germania quoque et Italia illa Langobardica imperii Romani nomine audiat, sequius quid est colligere. Familiare enim est et receptum, si multae respublicae coeant in unum foedus, ab una aliqua illarum omnibus nomen commune indere. Ita olim Achaeorum respublica omnibus foederatis nomen dedit, et urbs Romana omnibus sociis. Hodie foederati omnes Helvetii ab uno pago Sviceri, foederatae item omnes Belgico-Germanicae provinciae vulgo Hollandiae nomine usurpantur. Eadem vero ratione et imperii Romani nomen sociis rebuspublicis esse inditum, vel haec verba indicaverint Gotfridi Viterbiensis. Hic, cum narrasset, Lotharium imperatorem regni sui tres in partes divisi partem unam, Italiam scilicet, cum imperatorio nomine maiori natu filio tribuisse, addit: *vide ad quantum defectum Romanum imperium devenerit, ut in tres partes diviso regno Francorum tertiae partis tertia pars esset imperium.* Apud alios scriptores tempore Caroli Calvi Gallia imperii nomine intelligitur, exclusa Germania. Otto Frisingensis, cum egisset de divisione regni Francici inter filios Ludovici Pii instituta, ita loquitur *libro 5. capitulo 35.: ex hinc diviso regno regna modo duo orientale et occidentale (quorum alterum* (orientale) *partem Ludovici ac Lotharii, sedemque regni Francorum, palatium Aquisgrani, ac imperium urbis Romae habet, aliud vero* (occidentale), *quod adhuc Francorum, eo quod istud Romanorum vocatur, appellatum, partem Caroli tenet) inveniuntur.* Unde

[D.c. First conclusion: The emperor has no right to rule Germany and Italy]

XLII. Now, since all of this is absolutely certain, there is no reason why we should not openly pronounce the following conclusion: *Germany and the Lombard kingdom of Italy are not true parts of the Roman empire, but separate states. Hence the emperor is not head or magistrate of the kingdoms of Germany and Lombardy in so far as he is emperor, but only in so far as he is king at the same time.*

[D.c.i. Objections from the common usage of the term "Roman empire"]

Nor can any different conclusion be drawn from the fact that Germany and Lombard Italy have for centuries been commonly referred to as the Roman empire. For it is a familiar and well-established fact that a single state can give its name to many states in common if they have entered into a confederation. Thus the state of the Achaeans once gave its name to all of its confederates, and the city of Rome to all of its allies. Today all confederate Helvetians are named after the canton of Schwyz alone, and all of the confederate Belgian-German provinces are commonly referred to as Holland. For the same reason the name of the Roman empire was given to states that were allied with it—or so it would appear from the words of Geoffrey of Viterbo. For having explained how Emperor Lothar gave one of the three parts into which he had divided his kingdom, namely Italy, together with the imperial title to his eldest son, he adds: "Look how the Roman empire had become so enfeebled that after the division of the Frankish realm into three parts the empire had now been reduced to a third of a third."[113] At the time of Charles the Bald other writers[114] identified the empire with France, not Germany. Otto of Freising, book five, chapter thirty-five, on the other hand, says the following, after having dealt with the division of the Frankish kingdom between the sons of Louis the Pious: "Because of this division of the realm there are now two kingdoms, an eastern one and a western one. One of these (the eastern one) contains the shares of Louis and Lothar, the seat of the kingdom of the Franks at the palace of Aix-la-Chapelle, and the empire of the city of Rome, whereas the other (the western one) contains the share of Charles and is still called kingdom of the Franks, because the former one is called the kingdom of the Romans."[115] Here we can see that by

---

[113] Godefridus Viterbiensis, "Pantheon," in *Scriptores*, ed. G. Waitz, Monumenta Germaniae Historica (Hannover: Hahn, 1872), 22:107–307, here part. 23, chap. 20. See also *PL* 198:875–1044, here 948A.

[114] I am not sure to whom Conring was referring here.

[115] Otto of Freising, *Chronica*, bk. 5, chap. 35.

perspicere est, iam aetate Friderici Barbarossae Germanicum et Langobardicum regnum vocatum vulgo regnum Romanorum, ita tamen, ut non lateret distinctio inter illa regna et imperium urbis Romae.

XLIII. Igitur ex illo nomine Romani imperii quidem haud licet colligere, Langobardicum et Germanicum regnum pertinere reapse ad imperium Romanum. Neglexerunt autem diu et ipsi reges Germanici imperatorio titulo regnorum Germaniae et Italiae memoriam adiicere, forte quod mos saeculi non ferret cumulum titulorum, nomen autem caesareum ea aetate adeo haberetur magnificum, ut adiicere quidquam videretur indecens. Constat sane eos nec adiecisse titulos ducatuum et comitatuum, quos tamen una cum regia et imperatoria dignitate possidebant. Primus, quantum videtur, Fridericus II. praeter caesareum nomen Siciliae et Hierosolymae titulum usurpavit,[xxvi] Svevici tamen ducatus titulo non adiecto. Eum imitatus centum et quinquaginta fere annis post Carolus IV. et Romanorum imperator semper augustus et Bohemiae rex voluit dici. Eius filius Sigismundus et imperator et Hungariae et Bohemiae rex audivit. Fridericus III. non multo post adiecit plurima propter ducatus, comitatus, et alias provincias sibi subditas, Germanici licet imperii feuda essent. Qui mos ab eo usque tempore invaluit. Maximilianus porro et Germaniae rex voluit dici, non tantum optimo iure sed et utilissimo instituto. Secuti autem Maximilianum ea in re sunt Carolus V. et omnes quotquot in hunc diem ab ea aetate Germaniae praefuerunt. Posset autem eodem iure et Italici (immo, ut alibi ostenditur, et Burgundici aut Arelatensis) regni titulus usurpari, quantum ex superioribus est manifestum. Nec vero idipsum non esset magno cum reipublicae bono coniunctum, quo unicuivis possit eo rectius constare tota reipublicae natura. Certe interest rerumpublicarum[xxvii] ad tuenda iura singularum ut, etiamsi unum principem acceperint, nomina prisca ne obliterentur.

[xxvi] 1674: "Siciliae et Hierosolymae regnum tum usurpavit."
[xxvii] 1674: "interest rerumpublicarum coniunctarum."

the age of Frederick Barbarossa the German and Lombard kingdoms were already commonly called kingdom of the Romans, but without obliterating the distinction between those kingdoms and the empire of the city of Rome.

[D.c.ii. Objections from the titles used by the kings of Germany and Italy]

XLIII. It is therefore not permissible to infer from the usage of the term "Roman empire" that the Lombard and German kingdoms actually belonged to the Roman empire. It is true that for a long time the German kings themselves neglected to add any reference to the kingdoms of Germany and Italy to their imperial title, perhaps because the custom of the times did not allow the accumulation of titles, and because the imperial title was considered to be so outstanding that it would have seemed inappropriate to make any additions to it. They certainly failed to add the titles of their duchies and counties as well, even though they did possess these duchies and counties in conjunction with the royal and imperial dignity.

As far as can be seen Frederick II was the first to expand the imperial title by assuming the titles[116] of Sicily and Jerusalem without, however, adding his title to the duchy of Swabia. Almost one hundred and fifty years later Charles IV imitated him by wishing to be called "Roman emperor forever augustus and king of Bohemia." His son Sigismund was called "emperor and king of Hungary and Bohemia." Not much later Frederick III included in his title the many duchies, counties, and other provinces that were subject to him, even though they were fiefs of the German empire. That was the custom that prevailed from then on. Maximilian wanted to be called king of Germany as well, not only with the very best right but also for a most useful purpose. Charles V followed Maximilian in this practice, as did all others who ruled over Germany from then until now. The title of the Italian kingdom and, as is shown elsewhere, even that of Burgundy, or the kingdom of Arles, could have been added with the same right, as is evident from what was said above. That would in fact have been of great advantage to the state, because the nature of the state as a whole would thus have been clearer to everyone. In order to safeguard the rights of their individual members it is surely in the interest of states[117] not to obliterate the old titles, even if all of them are ruled by one and the same prince.

---

[116] In the version of 1674 Conring substituted "taking possession of the kingdoms" for "assuming the titles."

[117] In the version of 1674 Conring added "confederated" to "states."

XLIV. Quin igitur quasi ratum esto ac constitutum, *Germanicum et Italicum regnum distinctas esse respublicas ab eo, quod vere imperium Romanum est dicendum, nec imperatorem, in quantum est imperator, vel Germaniam regere vel Langobardicum regnum.* Hinc vero sequitur gravissime illos hallucinari, qui Germaniam censent teneri legibus Iustinianeis, aut imperatori in Germaniam arrogant potestatem priscorum caesarum in imperium Romanum eo nomine, quod Germania sit vere imperium Romanum et imperator, quatenus est imperator, Germaniae praesit. Utrumque sane esse longe falsissimum iam ostensum est. Non attingam enim nunc quam imbecillis sit illa collectio, etiamsi utrumque verum esset quod sumunt.

XLV. Non minus vero hinc liquet, quam inique papae Romani imperii nomine abusi rebus Germaniae sese immiscuerint easque perturbarint aliquot ante saeculis, quamve inique non adeo pridem Paulus IV. voluerit suas in manus resignari Romanum imperium, Gregorius vero XV. electoralem dignitatem Bavaro collatam confirmare. Habuit enim olim quidem papa Romanus una cum aliis civibus Romanis eligendi caesarem potestatem, et vero elegit ille et Carolum Magnum et post Ottonem Magnum. Sed in electionem regis Germaniae nihil umquam habuit iuris, iam Ottonum vero tempore etiam caesarum electionem in liberum Germaniae procerum arbitrium transtulit. Qua de re alibi. Certe, ut hodie etiam aliquid iuris sit papae in electionem caesaris (quod tamen est falsum), eo tamen nomine non debuit ille sui iuris quoque facere electionem regis Germaniae et Italiae.

XLVI. Porro et hoc consectaneum est: si iure potestas caesarem creandi possit Germaniae adimi, aut illa nollet aliquem creare, eo ipso tamen non amittere illam facultatem creandi regis Germanici et Italici regni. Ita, si licuisset Alexandro III.

[D.c.iii. Germany is a separate state from the Roman empire and not subject to Roman law]

XLIV. The following shall therefore be held to have been conclusively established: *The German and Italian kingdoms are distinct states from the Roman empire properly so called, and the emperor, in so far as he is emperor, rules neither Germany nor the Lombard kingdom.* It follows that those who maintain that Germany is bound by the laws of Justinian, and who claim that the emperor exercises the same power over Germany as the ancient emperors exercised over the Roman empire, on the grounds that Germany is truly identical with the Roman empire and that the emperor rules Germany in his capacity as emperor, suffer from serious delusions. For both of those grounds have now been demonstrated to be utterly false. And I am not going to point out how feeble their reasoning would be even if we were to grant the truth of both of their assumptions.

[D.d. Second conclusion: The papacy has no right to interfere in the affairs of Germany]

XLV. It is equally clear how grave an injustice the papacy committed when it abused the name of the Roman empire to interfere in the affairs of Germany and disturb them several centuries ago; when only very recently Paul IV wanted the Roman empire to be resigned into his hands; and when Gregory XV wanted to confirm the conferral of the electoral dignity on Bavaria.

[D.d.i. Objections from the papacy's right to elect the emperor]

It is true that once upon a time the Roman pope had the power to elect the emperor along with the other Roman citizens. Thus he elected both Charlemagne and later Otto the Great. But he never had any right to elect the king of Germany, and as early as the time of the Ottonians he also transferred his right to elect the emperor to the free judgment of the German nobles. About which more is said elsewhere. But even if it were granted that the pope continues to have some right to elect the emperor (which is false) he would still not be entitled to elect the kings of Germany and Italy as well.

[D.d.ii. Objections from the papacy's right to transfer the empire to other rulers]

XLVI. And this also follows: even if the power to choose the emperor can legally be taken away from Germany, or if Germany refuses to make anyone emperor, Germany cannot for that reason alone lose the power to choose the kings of Germany and Italy. Assuming that Pope Alexander III had the right to transfer

papae imperii occidentalis dignitatem in Constantinopolitanos iterum transferre, quod rogasse Emmanuelem caesarem scribit Blondus *libro 5. decadum 2.* et Platina *in vita Alexandri III.*, aut vero si Bonifacius VIII. iure potuisset promissis stare (pollicitus autem erat se imperii dignitatem in Gallos translaturum), non tamen ea propter iure potuisset Germaniae et Italiae respublica ab iis in alios transferri.

XLVII. Denique et hoc sequitur, non esse, cur nonnulli adeo pertendant, imperii Romani dignitatem non esse a Romano papa collatam vel Carolo Magno vel Ottone, eo quod uterque iam ante coronationem Germaniam ac Italiam possederit. Non enim est difficile probatu, factum id omnino esse a papa et populo Romano. Sed quod collatum fuit, id vero, si cum Germania et Italia Langobardica contendas, paene est nihil. Certe non est, cur hac de causa sese iactitent Romani pontifices, quasi scilicet magno beneficio Germaniam affecerint, utpote cum, si rem videas, potius opinione collatio illa insigne quid habet quam reapse. Verum de toto hoc negotio non est huius loci latius agitare.

XLVIII. Ceterum, cum nec Germania nec Italia Langobardica subsit hodie imperatori, ut ille est Romanus caesar, ergo aut reliquum omne Italiae illi isthoc nomine paret, aut aliquid eius, aut vero nihil. Ostensum autem est supra, cum

the dignity of the western empire back to the Constantinopolitans, as Emperor Emmanuel[118] is said to have requested according to Flavio Biondo, *Decades*, decade two, book five,[119] and Platina in his *Life of Alexander III*,[120] or that Boniface VIII had the right to keep his promise to transfer the imperial dignity to the French, they would still not have had the right to transfer the states of Germany and Italy from Germans to anyone else.

[D.d.iii. The insignificance of the role of the papacy]

XLVII. Finally it follows that there is no reason for anyone to insist that the Roman pope did not confer the dignity of the Roman empire on Charlemagne and Otto on the grounds that Charlemagne and Otto were in control of Germany and Italy well before their coronations. For it is not difficult to prove that the pope and the people of Rome did indeed confer the imperial dignity on them. But if you compare the worth of what they conferred with that of Germany and Lombard Italy, it amounts almost to nothing. It is certainly no reason for the Roman bishops to boast, as if they had done Germany some great favor. If you look at the facts, their conferral derives its significance from opinion rather than from reality. But this is not the place to pursue this matter any further.

[E. Does the Roman empire still exist today?]

XLVIII. Furthermore, since the emperor in his capacity as Roman emperor rules neither Germany nor Lombard Italy today, the empire must extend to the rest of Italy, to a part of the rest of Italy, or to nothing at all.

---

[118] Manuel I Comnenus. See also A. Kazhdan, "Alexander III," in *Oxford Dictionary of Byzantium*, 1:57, and C. M. Brand et al., "Manuel I Komnenos," 2:1289–90.

[119] Flavio Biondo, *Historiarum ab inclinatione Romanorum imperii libri xxxi* (Basileae: Froben, 1559), decade 2, bk. 5, 251. Cf. Flavio Biondo, *Le decadi*, trans. Achille Crespi (Castrocaro Terme: Comune di Forlì, 1963), bk. 15, chap. 23, 406; note that the numbering of books and chapters in Crespi's translation does not correspond to the decades and books in Froben's 1559 edition. My thanks to J. Michael Raley for verifying this reference.

[120] Bartolomeo Platina, *De vitis pontificum Romanorum, a D. N. Iesu Christo usque ad Paulum II*. (Coloniae Agrippinae: Ex officina Choliniana, 1626), 191–95, for the life of Alexander III. The embassy from Byzantium is mentioned on 192. See also Bartolomeo Platina, *Liber de vita Christi ac omnium pontificum*, ed. G. Gaida, Rerum Italicarum Scriptores 3.1 (Città di Castello: Lapi, 1913–1932). Cf. Bartolomeo Platina, *The Lives of the Popes from the Time of Our Saviour Jesus Christ to the Death of Paul II*, ed. William Benham, trans. Paul Rycaut, 2 vols., The Ancient and Modern Library of Theological Literature (London: Griffith, Farran, Okeden & Welsh, 1888).

Carolus Magnus imperii rerum est potitus, tum ex pacto Calabriam inferiorem mansisse in ditione imperii orientalis, Venetorum quoque urbem iisdem redditam, reliquum autem omne, utut pareret pontifici, in Caroli ut imperatoris supremam potestatem pervenisse. Fuit autem et Ottonis eadem prope conditio. Namque et tum nihil reliquum relictum est orientali imperio praeter Calabriam. Venetorum vero urbs itidem mansit libera. Cetera vero omnia imperii veteris in Italia, tametsi essent in pontificis manu, una tamen cum ipso pontifice in Ottonis ut caesaris imperium pervenerunt. Luitprandus, sive alius quis auctor eorum quae a capite sexto sunt assumpta *libri 6. Luitprandi,* scribit Ottonem ab Ioanne papa unctionem suscepisse imperii, addens: *iusiurandum vero ab eodem papa Ioanne supra pretiosissimum corpus Petri atque ab omnibus civitatis proceribus, se numquam Berengario atque Alberto auxiliaturos, accepit.* Otto imperator *capitulo 10.* conqueritur, Ioannem papam esse *immemorem iuramenti et fidelitatis, quam sibi supra corpus S. Petri promiserit.* Unde claret papam *fidelitatem* iurasse imperatori Ottoni, quae vox, quam habeat vim, ex more eius aevi notum est. In diplomate Ottonis illius Ioanni pontifici dato de bonis episcopatus Romani apud Baronium *ad annum 962.* diserte bona illa omnia donantur, sed hac conditione: *salva in omnibus potestate nostra et filii nostri posterorumque nostrorum.* Item ne quis pontifex imposterum consecraretur (verba caesaris sunt), *priusquam talem in praesentia missorum nostrorum, vel filii nostri, seu universae generalitatis faciat promissionem pro omnium satisfactione atque futura*

[E.a. The extent of imperial power from Charlemagne to the present]

[E.a.i. From Charlemagne to Otto the Great]

Now it has been shown above that, at the time when Charlemagne acquired the empire, a treaty left Calabria Inferior in control of the eastern empire and Venice was returned to the Venetians while the rest of Italy, inasmuch as it obeyed the pope, fell under the supreme power of Charles in his capacity as Roman emperor. It has also been shown that under Otto the Great conditions were basically the same. For at that time, too, nothing was left to the eastern empire except Calabria while Venice continued to enjoy its liberty as before. All the other parts of the old empire in Italy, however, though they were in the hands of the pope, fell together with the pope himself under Otto's power in his capacity as Roman emperor.

Liudprand, or whoever else is the author of the contents of chapter six of Liudprand's sixth book, writes that Otto was anointed to the empire by Pope John and then adds: "He took an oath from Pope John on the most precious body of Peter, and from all the nobles of the city, that they would never help Berengar and Albert."[121] In chapter ten Emperor Otto complains that Pope John "does not remember the oath and fealty which he vowed on the body of Saint Peter."[122] This shows that the pope swore fealty to Emperor Otto, and we know from the custom of that age how much that term meant. In the charter about the goods of the Roman bishopric that Otto granted to Pope John, quoted by Baronio for the year 962, all of these goods are explicitly granted on the condition that "our power, that of our son, and that of our successors shall remain undiminished in every respect" and that, in the emperor's words, no one should henceforth be consecrated pope "until he has vowed in the presence of our envoys, our son, or the entire community to fulfill and keep in the future all of the promises that our reverend

---

[121] Liudprand of Cremona, "Liber de Ottone rege," in *Quellen zur Geschichte der Sächsischen Kaiserzeit*, ed. and trans. Bauer and Rau, 496–523, here chap. 3. See also André Duchesne, *Historiae Francorum scriptores*, 5 vols. (Parisiis: Sumptibus S. Cramoisy, 1636–1649), 3:627–34, and *PL* 136:898–910. Cf. *The Works of Liudprand of Cremona*, trans. Wright, 213–32. The attribution of this text to Liudprand was not undisputed. Baronio, *Annales ecclesiastici*, discussing its authorship at the beginning of year 963, concluded that it was not by Liudprand. Conring left the question open. The modern edition numbers the chapters differently from early modern editions like the one on which Conring relied. In André Duchesne's edition, the text was not only divided into longer chapters but also appended as chapters six to eleven to the end of the sixth book of Liudprand's *Antapodosis*.

[122] Liudprand of Cremona, "Liber de Ottone rege," chap. 15, in the modern numbering.

conservatione, qualem dominus et venerandus spiritualis pater noster Leo sponte fecisse dignoscetur. Atqui Leo illi Carolo Magno subiecit sese, prout olim caesaribus fuere subiecti papae, eoque Carolum statim adoravit, quod iam supra est dictum. In eodem porro diplomate notandum illud est, conventum tum esse, ut quotannis per legatos caesari nuncietur, *qualem singuli duces ac iudices populo iustitiam faciant.* Si enim sequius quid fiat quam oportet, tum vero imperatorem per legatos suos id emendaturum.

XLIX. Ex quibus profecto liquet, statim illo anno 962. Ottonem una cum caesareo titulo iura veterum caesarum in papam ipsum accepisse. Et vero eo iure usus est contra Ioannem illum papam statim sequente anno. Quo tempore de novo cives Romani *fidelitatem* promiserunt, *haec addentes* (verba sunt Luitprandi loco citato) *et firmiter iurantes, numquam se papam electuros et ordinaturos praeter consensum atque electionem domini imperatoris Ottonis caesaris augusti filiique ipsius regis Ottonis.* Rogavit autem tum synodus episcoporum ab Ottone congregata, ut et Ioannem papam exuere honore et alium in eius locum eligi pateretur. Utrumque autem effectum est. Eidem vero Ottoni Romani cives periuri 964. et tertia vice *fidelitatem* iurarunt, ut post Reginonem narrat Baronius. Quo anno iterum caesarea auctoritate usus Otto in exilium relegavit Benedictum, quem Romani cives crearant pontificem. Eidem porro Ottoni omnibusque eius successoribus Leo papa praeter illa iam dicta concessit *in perpetuum facultatem eligendi successorem* (in imperio scilicet) *atque summae sedis apostolicae pontificem ordinandi, ac per hoc archiepiscopos seu episcopos, ut ipsi ab eo investituram accipiant.* Habentur omnia haec verba ex bulla quadam Leonis deprompta apud ipsum Gratianum *distinctione 63. capitulo 23.* Exstat quoque apud Crancium *metropolis libro 4. capitulo 10.* eiusdem Leonis alia bulla, qua omnia quae Pipinus aut Carolus Magnus donaverant Romanae ecclesiae Ottoni eiusque successoribus redduntur. Impugnat vero acriter utriusque fidem Baronius *ad annum 964.* Quicquid vero sit de illis bullis, id certum est, Leone mortuo ius illud eligendi ex arbitrio pontificem non

spiritual father Lord Leo is known to have made on his own accord." And what is more, Pope Leo III submitted himself to Charlemagne in the same way in which popes subjected themselves to emperors in antiquity, honoring Charles with a ceremonial adoration immediately after his coronation, as has been pointed out above. Note that in the same charter it was also agreed that every year the emperor was to be informed by legates "how the dukes and judges were rendering justice to the people." For if anything had gone amiss, the emperor was going to correct it through legates.

XLIX. That proves that when Otto accepted the imperial title in 962 he thereby acquired the rights of the ancient emperors over the pope. And in the very next year he used those rights against Pope John. At that time the citizens of Rome promised Otto their fealty once again and, in the words of Liudprand, "added and swore firm oaths never to elect and ordain a pope without the consent and against the choice of Lord Emperor Otto Caesar Augustus and his son King Otto."[123] The episcopal synod assembled by Otto then asked him to give them his permission to deprive Pope John of his honor and to elect someone else in his place. Both things were done. When the citizens of Rome violated their oath to Otto in 964, they swore fealty for yet a third time, as Baronio reports following Regino.[124] In that year Otto relied on his imperial authority once again to send Pope Benedict into exile, whom the Roman citizens had elected pope. In addition to all of this Pope Leo granted Otto and all of his successors "the right forever to choose his successor (that is, to the empire) and to ordain the bishop of the highest apostolic see, and the archbishops and bishops accordingly, so that they would accept their investiture from the emperor."

All of these words are contained in a bull obtained from Leo and cited by Gratian himself in distinction sixty-three, chapter twenty-three.[125] In Krantz, *Metropolis*, book four, chapter ten,[126] there is another bull of Leo, in which everything donated to the Roman Church by Pipin or Charlemagne is returned to Otto and his successors. Baronio, for the year 964, sharply disputes the authenticity of both of these bulls. But whatever may be the case with these bulls, certain is that when Pope Leo died the Romans were fully aware of the emperor's right to

---

[123] Liudprand of Cremona, "Liber de Ottone rege," chap. 8.

[124] More precisely, following Adalbert's "Continuatio Reginonis," year 964.

[125] Gratian, *Decretum*, ed. E. Friedberg, in *Corpus Iuris Canonici* (Leipzig: B. Tauchnitz, 1879), 1:241.

[126] The reference is not to Krantz's *Ecclesiastica historia, sive Metropolis*, cited above, chap. 31, but to the same author's *Saxonia et metropolis* (Coloniae: Apud Gerwinum Calenium & haeredes Quentelios, 1574), bk. 4, chap. 10. Krantz does mention the charter in question in bk. 3, chap. 33 of the *Ecclesiastica historia, sive Metropolis*, but for the full text of the charter he refers readers to his *Saxonia et metropolis*.

latuisse Romanos. Continuator Reginonis *ad annum 965.* ita notat: *eodem anno dominus papa Leo obiit. Tunc legati Romanorum imperatorum pro instituendo, quem vellent,*[xxviii] *Romano pontifice in Saxonia adeuntes honorifice suscipiuntur et remittuntur. Et Otgarus Spirensis episcopus et Luitprandus Cremonensis cum iisdem Romam ab imperatore diriguntur. Tunc ab omni plebe Romana Ioannes eligitur.* Immo ex eo usque tempore omnes pontifices Romani, aliique archiepiscopi pariter, et episcopi pedum episcopale ab imperatoribus acceperunt, donec rem omnem turbaret Gregorius VII. Id quod alibi ostenditur.

 L. Quin itaque Otto Magnus vere caesaream obtinuerit in pontificem populumque Romanum potestatem, non est dubitandum. Potest autem de successoribus eiusdem ad Henricum IV. usque idem haud difficulter ostendi, si opus foret. Verum id operose agere fuerit forte soli facem faenerari. De Ottone III. tamen quae dicit Glaber Rodulphus non possumus praetermittere. *Contigit,* ait, *initio imperii Ottonis, ut sedes apostolica urbis Romae proprio viduaretur pontifice* (is erat Ioannes XV.), *ipse vero illico imperiali usus praecepto quendam suum consanguineum* (Brunonem, post dictum Gregorium V.) *elegit, atque ex more in sede apostolica sublimari mandavit.* Cum vero eodem tempore Crescentius consul tyrannidem[xxix] urbis sibi sumpsisset aliumque pontificem instituisset, narrat idem, atque ex eo Baronius *ad annum 996.,* Ottonem et urbem occupasse et Crescentium curasse praecipitari, papae autem a Crescentio electo et manus amputatas, et aures abscissas, et oculos erutos. Idem ille Otto Sylvestrum II. papam instituit fatente Baronio anno 999. Idem Otto Sylvestro papae octo urbes marchiae Anconitanae donavit. Refert illud Theodoricus de Niem *libro de privilegiis et iuribus imperii.* Ipsum vero donationis

---

 [xxviii] 1674: "*Tunc legati Romanorum imperatorem pro instituendo quem vellet.*"
 [xxix] 1674: "principatum."

choose a pope according to his own free decision. As the continuator of Regino points out for 965: "Pope Leo died in the same year. Legates of the Roman emperors then went to Saxony in order to appoint someone to their liking as bishop of Rome.[127] They were received with honor and sent back again, and the emperor chose Bishop Otgar of Speyer and Liudprand of Cremona to accompany them to Rome. Then John was elected pope by the entire Roman people." Thereafter every bishop of Rome as well as the other archbishops and bishops received the episcopal staff from the emperor, until Gregory VII threw everything into turmoil. Which is shown elsewhere.

[E.a.ii. From Otto the Great to Henry IV]

L. There is no doubt, therefore, that Otto the Great truly obtained imperial power over the bishop and people of Rome. If it were necessary, the same could without difficulty be shown to be true for his successors down to Henry IV. To spend any effort on doing so, however, would amount to lending a torch to the sun. Still, I cannot pass over what Rodulfus Glaber says about Otto III: "It happened at the beginning of Otto's rule as emperor," he says, "that the apostolic see of Rome lost its bishop (that is, John XV). Under the circumstances Otto relied on the imperial precept to choose one of his relatives (Bruno, later called Gregory V) and ordered his elevation to the apostolic see according to custom."[128] But since Consul Crescentius had at the same time established his tyranny[129] over the city and set up someone else as pope, he reports—and Baronio follows him for the year 996—that Otto occupied the city and took care to have Crescentius overthrown, while the pope chosen by Crescentius had his hands and ears cut off and his eyes torn out. The same Otto III, as Baronio writes for 999, appointed Sylvester II as pope. He also gave Pope Sylvester eight cities of the March of Ancona. Dietrich of Niem reports this in his *Book on the Privileges and Rights of the Empire*.[130] Marquard Freher was the first to edit the charter of

---

[127] Adalbert, "Continuatio Reginonis," year 965. This sentence is neither accurately quoted nor does it make much sense as it stands in the *New Discourse* and the *Exercitatio* of 1641. In the version of 1674 Conring corrected it as follows: "Roman legates then approached the emperor in Saxony in order to appoint someone to his liking as bishop of Rome."

[128] Rodulfus Glaber, *Historiarum libri quinque. The Five Books of the Histories*, ed. and trans. John France (Oxford: Oxford University Press, 1989), here bk. 1, chap. 12. See also *PL* 142:611–698, here 620D–621A.

[129] In the version of 1674 Conring replaced "tyranny" with "principate."

[130] Dietrich of Niem, "Privilegia aut iura imperii circa investituras episcopatuum et abbatiarum restituta a papis imperatoribus Romanis," in Simon Schard, *De iurisdictione, autoritate, et praeeminentia imperiali ac potestate ecclesiastica* (Basileae: Oporinus, 1566), 785–859, here 832.

diploma edidit primus Marquardus Freherus et insigni commentario illustravit; post illum a Baronio id *tomo 12. annalium ad annum 1191.* est insertum. Liquet vero inde, eo tempore magnum illud quod appellatur Petri patrimonium non in pontificis sed in imperatoris fuisse manibus, forte quod Leo omne illud Ottoni Magno iterum concessisset. In illis autem litteris notatu etiam hoc occurrit dignum, quod Romam appellet caesar *suam urbem regiam.* Huius porro Ottonis adhuc pueri mater Theophane per triennium ipsa Romae vixit et rempublicam filii sui in usum tenuit. Quomodo anno 1033. Conradus II. integrum annum Romae commoratus rebelles compescuit.

LI. Quamquam vero haec vera caesarea potestas integra manserit ad Henricum usque Quartum (cuius pater Henricus III. adeo iure suo est usus, ut non dubitaverit Baronius anno 1046. illum hoc nomine nescio cuius haereseos Henricianae auctorem proclamare), immo quamquam ipse Gregorius VII. papa confirmari voluerit per Henricum IV., primus tamen ille inaudito hactenus scelere non tantum exuere caesarem omni dignitate est ausus, sed et sumere sibi potestatem in imperatorem, reges, principes. Presserunt autem eiusdem vestigia omnes secuti pontifices. Quamquam vero strenue iura sua antiqua tueri ac servare studuerint cum ipse Henricus IV., tum eius filius Henricus V., nec non Fridericus primus et secundus, tandem tamen post obitum scilicet Friderici II. impietas[xxx] paparum victoriam expressit. Igitur iam quidem annos prope quadringentos neque in papam, neque in urbem Romam, neque in illas antiqui imperii reliquas provincias caesarea vetus potentia[xxxi] fuit exercita. Superstes tantum mansit imperatorium nomen et quidem, si verum est dicendum, inane atque procul re ipsa.[xxxii] Quod

---

[xxx] 1674: "violentia."
[xxxi] 1674: "antiqui imperii reliquias caesarum pristina quidem iusta potentia."
[xxxii] 1674: "ferme inane atque procul re ipsa, quantum quidem stetit penes curiam papalem."

this donation and to illustrate it with an excellent commentary.[131] Following him, Baronio included it in volume twelve of his *Annals* for the year 1191.[132] Hence it is clear that the great so-called Patrimony of Peter was not in the hands of the pope at that time, but in those of the emperor, possibly because Leo had returned all of it to Otto the Great. It is also worth noting that the emperor calls Rome "his royal city" in those letters. When Otto III was still a boy, furthermore, his mother Theophanu[133] lived for three years in Rome and ruled the state for her son's use. Conrad II similarly checked a rebellion against himself by residing in Rome for an entire year in 1033.

[E.a.iii. From Pope Gregory VII to the present]

LI. This genuinely imperial power remained intact down to the time of Emperor Henry IV. His father, Henry III, still exercised his rights in the year 1046 in such a manner that Baronio did not hesitate to pronounce him the author of some Henrician heresy that I have never heard of.[134] Even Pope Gregory VII himself wanted to be confirmed by Henry IV. But at the same time Gregory VII was also the first who dared to commit the unheard-of crime, not only of stripping the emperor of all dignity, but also of assuming power over emperor, kings, and princes for himself. And all later pontiffs followed in his tracks. Henry IV and his son Henry V as well as Frederick I and Frederick II tried strenuously to protect and preserve their ancient rights. But in the end, after the death of Frederick II, the godlessness[135] of the popes wrested victory from the emperors. Hence close to four hundred years have now passed since the old[136] imperial power was last exercised over the pope, the city of Rome, and the other provinces of the ancient Roman empire. What remains is only the imperial name and, if truth be told, that name is now[137] worthless and has no bearing on the real state of affairs.[138]

---

[131] Marquard Freher, *Constantini magni imperatoris donatio Sylvestro papae Romano inscripta* (Heidelberg: Typis G. Voegelini, 1610). The commentaries in this book have also been attributed to Isaac Casaubon.

[132] Volume 19 in the edition I used. Conring neglected to mention that Baronio disputed the authenticity of the charter.

[133] See C. M. Brand et al., "Theophano," in *Oxford Dictionary of Byzantium* 3:2065; and *The Empress Theophano: Byzantium and the West at the Turn of the First Millennium*, ed. Adelbert Davids (Cambridge: Cambridge University Press, 1995), with further reading on xii–xiii.

[134] Baronio, *Annales ecclesiastici*, year 1046, recounting the events of the synod of Sutri.

[135] In the version of 1674 Conring substituted "violence" for "godlessness."

[136] In the version of 1674 Conring added "and just."

[137] In the version of 1674 Conring added "almost."

[138] In the version of 1674 Conring added "inasmuch as it is under the control of the papal curia."

iam olim recte intellexit fortissimus Germanicorum caesarum Fridericus primus eoque, cum Adrianus IV. papa anno 1159. inter alia a Friderico posceret, *nuncios ad urbem ignorante apostolico ab imperatore non esse mittendos, cum omnis magistratus inibi S. Petri sit cum universis regalibus,* statim respondit, *cum divina ordinatione ego Romanus imperator et dicar et sim, speciem tantum dominantis effingo et inane ubique porto nomen ac sine re, si urbis Romae de manu nostra potestas fuerit excussa.*

LII. Non disputabo nunc, an quadringentorum annorum possessione id, quod initio per vim et scelera peperunt sibi, pontifices nunc vere suum fecerint, praesertim cum tanto temporis spacio pauci caesares idipsum videantur in controversiam vocasse. Id certum videtur:[xxxiii] si tot annorum praescriptione perierint nostris regibus et caesaribus omnia vera illa et antiqua caesarum iura,[xxxiv] non esse amplius, cur vane iactent nonnulli nescio quod orbis aut urbis Romae dominium, multo minus[xxxv] nunc esse magnis sumptibus et ingenti periculo in Italiam proficiscendum caesaribus electis, quo a Romano pontifice caesaream coronam consequantur. Quin immo haud obscure hinc est dispicere, cum orientale imperium Romanorum per Turcam pridem sit destructum, nec occidentalis quidquam paene supersit apud caesares praeter nomen imperatorium, haud iniuria fortassis posse affirmari, vel imperium Romanum funditus periisse, vel vero papam Romanum reapse frui nunc potestate imperatoria, si demas licentiam titulum illum usurpandi aut in alium conferendi.

LIII. Ceterum his quae ultimo attulimus nonnulla posse obiici videntur. Primo enim sacris litteris videtur praedictum, non interiturum Romanum imperium ante ultimum diem. Ex legibus quoque Iustinianeis constat imperatorem dominum esse orbis. Certum vero est nostros caesares Iustiniani esse successores.

[xxxiii] 1674: "id certum haud forte iniuria videtur."
[xxxiv] 1674: "caesarum iura (quod tamen neutiquam admitti potest)."
[xxxv] 1674: "multo minus fortasse."

Long ago Frederick I, the most powerful among German emperors, already understood precisely what was at stake. In 1159, when Pope Hadrian IV demanded from him, among other things, "not to send any messengers to the city of Rome without the knowledge of the pope, because the magistracies and the regalia of Rome belong entirely to St. Peter,"[139] he responded immediately: "Although I am called Roman emperor by divine ordination, and am so in fact, I would be a mere fiction of a ruler and carry an empty name without any substance if power over the city of Rome were to be struck from my hand."[140]

[E.b. Third conclusion: The Roman empire has either ceased to exist completely or it is in the hands of the papacy]

LII. I am not now going to analyze whether four hundred years of possession is enough for the popes to have acquired a genuine right over what they first took by force and crime, especially since in all of that time few emperors seem to have disputed the case. But this, at least, seems certain:[141] if after so many years of prescription our kings and emperors have lost all those true and ancient rights of the emperors,[142] there is no longer any reason why some of them should vainly boast, I do not know what kind of lordship over the world or the city of Rome, much less,[143] why emperors-elect should at great expense and overwhelming danger march into Italy in order to obtain the imperial crown from the Roman bishop. The conclusion is not difficult to perceive: since the eastern Roman empire has long since been destroyed by the Turks and hardly anything of the western empire is left to our emperors except the imperial title, it is perhaps not wrong to affirm that either the Roman empire has perished completely or, if you put aside the question of whether or not the papacy had the right to usurp the imperial title and confer it on others, that the imperial power is now actually in the hands of the Roman pope.

LIII. Now, several objections can apparently be made against what we just stated. First, Sacred Scripture seems to predict that the Roman empire will not perish until the end of the world. Second, according to the laws of Justinian the emperor is lord of the world. Since our emperors surely are the successors of Justinian, they

---

[139] Rahewin, *Gesta Frederici*, bk. 4, chap. 34, trans. Mierow and Emery, 269.

[140] Rahewin, *Gesta Frederici*, bk. 4, chap. 35, trans. Mierow and Emery, 271.

[141] In the version of 1674 Conring substituted the more cautious "this, at least, does not seem to be wrong" for the more forceful "this, at least, seems certain."

[142] In the version of 1674 Conring added in parentheses: "which cannot be admitted by any means." This of course turns the argument on its head. For the significance of this change see Fasolt, "Author and Authenticity," esp. 211–12.

[143] In the version of 1674 Conring added "perhaps."

Itaque et nostris illis in orbem quoque universum eadem hodie iura sunt. Postremo, si caesares hodie reapse non nisi imperatorium habent titulum, haud videtur eorum esse aliqua prae aliis regibus dignitas ac praerogativa.

LIV. Verum enimvero, quod primo quidem loco adducitur, promitti in sacris litteris imperii Romani aeternitatem, id temere probari non potest. Quomodo totum illud de non nisi quatuor magnis futuris monarchiis seu imperiis mundi plus habet famae quam veri, quippe cum olim in Asia iam ante Alexandrum tot numero floruerint amplissima imperia Assyriorum, Babyloniorum, Medorum, Persarum, non autem duo tantum, quod vulgo creditur. Asia eadem post Romani imperii interitum itidem habuerit, hodieque ex parte habeat, vastissima regna Sarracenorum, Turcarum, Tartarorum, Persarum, et Sinensium. Europa vero viderit Francorum regnum maximum iam ante adeptum caesareum nomen, etiam nunc vero floreant vasta Hispanorum potentia et Gallorum. Nec vero reperitur quid in sacris litteris, quod ad perpetuitatem Romani imperii iure debeat trahi. Sive enim somnium Nabuchodonosaris videas, sive ipsius Danielis quod est capitulo 7., omnia illa vix attingunt caesaria tempora, ut optime observant eruditiores, quod tamen hic disputare alienum est. Quid, quod apostolicae litterae excidium non Romani imperii tantum sed et ipsius urbis haud paulo ante finem mundi futurum videantur praedicere? Antichristi certe tempora excepta demum interitum Romani imperii, communis omnium primae aetatis Christianorum fuit sententia. De ipsius autem urbis Romae extremo excidio accipienda videntur omnino illa, quae capitulo 18. apocalypsi leguntur.

have the same rights over the whole world today. Third and last, if the emperors really have nothing except the imperial title today, there seems to be no dignity or prerogative that raises them above other kings.

[E.b.i. Objections from the Bible]

LIV. But the first objection, namely that Sacred Scripture promises eternity to the Roman empire, must not be blindly accepted. For the whole idea that there will be only four great monarchies or world empires is more of a rumor than a fact. Even before the arrival of Alexander the Great, four very large empires—and not only two, as is commonly believed—had already flourished in Asia: the Assyrian, Babylonian, Median, and Persian. And after the destruction of the Roman empire, Asia again gave rise to vast realms under Saracens, Turks, Tatars, Persians, and Chinese, as it still does to some extent today. In Europe, moreover, the realm of the Franks was huge well before Charles became emperor, and nowadays Spain and France are enjoying enormous power. Moreover, nothing in Sacred Scripture really establishes that the Roman empire will last forever, for neither the dream of Nebuchadnezzar[144] nor that of Daniel, chapter seven, have much to do with Roman imperial times, as the learned recognize very well. But this is not the place to analyze this question.

What about the point that the letters of the Apostles seem to predict that not only the empire, but also the city of Rome will perish shortly before the end of the world? The first Christians were certainly unanimous in their conviction that the times of Antichrist would begin with the destruction of the Roman empire. But as far as the final destruction of the city of Rome is concerned, it seems we ought to rely entirely on the statements of the Apocalypse, chapter eighteen.[145]

---

[144] Daniel 2.

[145] It is not altogether clear how to reconcile this interpretation of the letters of the Apostles, the Apocalypse, and early Christian beliefs with the main argument of the text. Here it seems to be granted that the end of the Roman empire will coincide with the end of the world. Yet the main argument of the text is that the Roman empire had already virtually ceased to exist. The parallel passage in the *De Germanorum imperio Romano*, chap. 11 par. 13–14, in *Opera*, 1:89–90, clarifies matters by distinguishing between the Roman empire properly speaking and the perverted version of the Roman empire controlled by the papacy and identical with the Roman church. The perverted version of the empire was Babylon. That was what would endure until the end of the world. See Irena Backus, *Reformation Readings of the Apocalypse: Geneva, Zurich and Wittenberg* (Oxford: Oxford University Press, 2000).

LV. Ad secundum respondemus. Eo argumenti genere usos quidem perquam multos a Lotharii caesaris usque temporibus ad nostram hanc aetatem eos, qui Romani iuris doctrinam professi sunt, quorum nonnullis paene persuasum est, omnia omnino illa competere hodieque caesaribus nostris, quae olim Iustiniano immo Augusto imperatori convenerunt. Verum haec quidem doctrina apta est concitandis bellis, movendis tumultibus, evertendae reipublicae.[xxxvi] Si enim omnia ad illam faciem augustaei aevi sunt componenda, non haec tantum nostra Germania, sed paene totus orbis erit commovendus. Est autem tota illa colligendi ratio frivola, ne quid dicam gravius. Nulla certe illi vis inest, nisi pro confesso et certo sumas, populum caesaremque Romanum nihil potuisse iure amittere, aut vero omne quod in corpore illo legum Romanarum reperitur, id ex iure naturae venire adeoque aeternae esse veritatis. Quae omnia longe sunt falsissima. Sane cum iura illa pleraque valeant ex constituto sintque positiva, uniuscuiusque est liberae reipublicae ea hactenus vel reiicere vel admittere, eoque nec rerumpublicarum controversiae recte ex illis possunt decidi, ut optime post Ferdinandum Vasquium observavit summus vir Hugo Grotius *praefatione ad librum de iure belli ac pacis*. Stultum vero est omnem, qui in nomen aut aliquo modo succedit in locum, eundem etiam in iura, quae ante aliquot centum aut mille annos obtinuerunt, succedere. Non minus sane hoc ineptum est, quam illud nonnullorum commentum, Carolo V. ius fuisse ad occupandos Americanos eo, quod esset imperator adeoque dominus orbis, quos perdocte confutavit Franciscus Victoria *relectione de Indis* et Ferdinandus Vasquius *in quaestionibus illustribus*. Bene vero est, quod qui sese olim caesarianarum partium propugnatoribus illis opposuerint, ac pontificem sumserint sibi extollendum *super omne quod dicitur deus,* non minus perperam sese gesserint, nihil aliud scilicet

---

[xxxvi] 1674: "evertendae etiam nostrae reipublicae."

[E.b.ii. Objections from Roman law]

LV. Concerning the second objection, I respond that this is precisely the kind of argument invoked by a great many professors of Roman law from the times of Emperor Lothar down to our own age. Some of them are almost completely convinced that whatever once belonged to Emperor Justinian or even to Augustus belongs in its entirety to our emperors today. Now that doctrine is certainly good for starting wars, promoting turmoil, and overturning the state.[146] For if everything must be arranged according to the manner of the age of Augustus, not only our Germany but nearly the whole world must be turned upside down.[147]

But that whole manner of reasoning is frivolous, to say nothing worse. It has no force whatsoever unless you assume as certain that there was no way for the people and emperor of Rome to lose any of their rights, or that every single piece in the body of Roman laws is founded on the law of nature and therefore true for all eternity. And that, of course, is totally false. Since most of those laws derive their validity from imperial constitutions and have the nature of positive law, it is up to each free state to reject or accept them. For the same reason controversies between states cannot be properly settled on the basis of those laws, as the great Hugo Grotius, following Fernando Vázquez, observes so well in the preface of *The Law of War and Peace*.

It is simply stupid to believe that whoever enters into someone else's place by name or in some other way also succeeds to rights that may have been in effect a hundred or a thousand years ago. It is in fact no less absurd than the opinion of those who pretend that Charles V had a right to occupy America because he was emperor and thus lord of the world.[148] Francisco de Vitoria refutes them with great learning in his *Lecture on the Indians*,[149] as does Fernando Vázquez in his *Famous Questions*.[150]

Truth to tell, those who fought against the champions of the imperial party in order to raise the pope above all because he was said to be God conducted them-

---

[146] In the version of 1674 Conring substituted "our state" for "the state."

[147] Note that, at least for the sake of polemics, in the present context Conring was willing to speak almost as loosely about "nearly the whole world" as the jurists whom he blamed for failing to realize the limits of the ancient Roman empire and its law.

[148] Actually Conring spoke of Charles V's pretended *ius . . . ad occupandos Americanos*, literally his "right to occupy the Americans," a formulation nicely reflecting a time of transition from identifying political power with power over people (as had been the case in medieval times) to identifying it with power over a territory (as came to be the case under the regime of sovereignty).

[149] See Francisco de Vitoria, *De Indis et De iure belli relectiones* (Washington, DC: Carnegie Institution, 1917). Cf. Francisco de Vitoria, *Political Writings*, ed. and trans. Anthony Pagden and Jeremy Lawrance (Cambridge: Cambridge University Press, 1991), 231–92.

[150] Vázquez, *Controversiarum illustrium . . . libri tres*, ed. and trans. Rodriguez.

adferentes quam ipsorum pontificum arrogantissima dicta, adeoque testimonium gloriosissimorum et superbissimorum nebulonum[xxxvii] in propria causa.

LVI. Tertii ultimique argumenti reiicienda est sequela. Enimvero non est caesari nostro quidquam potestatis in liberas respublicas, sed ratione αὐτονομίας etiam parva respublica libera, qualis est Rhegusina exempli gratia, non minus sua habet plena maiestatis iura quam aliqua magna. Dignitas vero omnis non ex illis maiestatis iuribus tantum est aestimanda, sed et alia multa sunt, quae iubeant etiam inter pares ordinem aliquem servandum. Certum vero est, Carolum Magnum cum Francis quoquovorsum imperium suum extendisse, in Germaniam scilicet et Galliam et Italiam et magnam Hispaniae partem, fuisse autem illos omnes natione et lingua Germanos, adeoque tum certe praecipuam Europae vim penes Germanos fuisse. Certum vero et hoc est: a tempore Ottonis Magni non tantum caesareo nomine sed et amplitudine imperii Germanicum regnum per complura saecula longe antecelluisse Hispaniam, Galliam, Britanniam, Daniam, Sveciam, Poloniam, Ungariam, utpote quae comprehenderet omnem Germaniam, Galliae magnam partem usque ad Rhodanum, regnum Arelatense, et Italiam universam. Denique certum est, ab annis septingentis nullam rempublicam non ultro semper Germaniae eiusque regibus aut caesaribus[xxxviii] primum locum concessisse. Itaque cum dignitas haec et προεδρία non tam a caesareo titulo quam ab ipsa amplitudine imperii veniat, et vero Germanicum regnum in quieta eius honoris possessione hactenus fuerit, manifestum est, etiam si tollas omne caesareum nomen, ius tamen suum[xxxix] Germanico regno permansurum integrum.

Finis.

[xxxvii] 1674: "superbissimorum aliquot paucorum hominum."
[xxxviii] 1674: "non ultro septem Germaniae regibus eiusque caesaribus."
[xxxix] 1674: "etiam si hodie tollatur omne imperatorium et imperii nomen (quod summum fuerit nefas), ius tantum suum."

selves no less badly, for they rested their case on nothing else than the most arrogant sayings of the popes themselves—which is to say, the testimony of[151] utterly vainglorious and domineering scoundrels[152] in their own cause.

[E.b.iii. Objections from the dignity of the emperor]

LVI. Finally, the conclusion drawn from the third objection is to be rejected. It is true that our emperor has no power whatsoever over any independent state, and that by virtue of its autonomy[153] even a small independent state as, for example, the republic of Ragusa, enjoys exactly the same rights of sovereignty[154] as a large one. But dignity must not be measured solely on the basis of rights of sovereignty, for there are many other rights that enjoin the observation of a certain order even among equals. Now it is a fact that Charlemagne and the Franks expanded their empire in every direction over Germany, France, Italy, and a great part of Spain. Since all of the Franks were German by nationality and language, the most eminent power in Europe surely lay with Germans at that time. It is also a fact that since the times of Otto the Great the kingdom of Germany excelled for several centuries above Spain, France, Britain, Denmark, Sweden, Poland, and Hungary, not only because of the imperial title but also because of the actual extent of its empire, which included all of Germany, a large part of France down to the Rhône, the kingdom of Arles, and all of Italy. Finally, there is no doubt that ever since the eighth century all other states have freely yielded first place to Germany and its kings or emperors.[155] Since this dignity and right of precedence[156] stem not so much from the imperial title as from the real extent of the empire, and since Germany's possession of this honor has heretofore not been contested, the rights of the German kingdom will clearly remain intact even if[157] you abolish the imperial title[158] totally.

The end.

---

[151] In the version of 1674 Conring added "a few."
[152] In the version of 1674 Conring substituted "men" for "scoundrels" (*nebulones*).
[153] Conring used the Greek αὐτονομία.
[154] *Maiestas* in the Latin.
[155] In the version of 1674 Conring changed this into "Germany's seven kings and its emperors."
[156] Conring used the Greek προεδρία.
[157] In the version of 1674 Conring added in parentheses: "which would be the greatest sacrilege." "Sacrilege" is *nefas* in the Latin, which implies offenses against divine, natural, and moral law all in one.
[158] In the version of 1674 Conring added "and the empire."

Corollaria:[xl]

I. Imperator, etiam in quantum est rex Germanorum, primarius est princeps Christiani orbis.

II. Regnum Germaniae semper fuit electitium, etsi usque ad tempora Henrici IV. semper ex parte habuerit aliquid hereditarii.

III. Regnum Germaniae mere electitium fuit redditum occasione tumultuum contra Henricum IV. excitatorum.

IV. Prior modus constituendi regem, qui aliquid[xli] admistum habet hereditarii, Germaniae rebus est convenientior altero illo pure electitio.

V. Regnum et imperium non in papae sed in electorum manus recte Carolus V. resignavit.

VI. Non est iure naturae vetitum usuram capere.

VII. Neque ius naturae obstat, quo minus magna oceani pars in privatam possit redigi possessionem.

[xl] The corollaries do not appear in the *New Discourse*. They do appear in the versions of 1641 and 1674.

[xli] 1674: "qui nempe aliquid."

Corollaries:[159]

1. The emperor, even in so far as he is king of Germany, is the first prince of the Christian world.

2. The kingdom of Germany was always elective, even though down to the times of Henry IV it had certain hereditary features.

3. The kingdom of Germany became purely elective because of the troubles raised against Henry IV.

4. The earlier way of establishing kings, namely the one with certain hereditary features, is more suited to German affairs than the purely elective one.

5. Charles V was right to resign the kingdom and the empire, not into the hands of the pope, but those of the electors.

6. Natural law does not prohibit the taking of interest.

7. Natural law does not object to turning a large part of the ocean over to private possession.

---

[159] The corollaries are taken from the *Exercitatio*. They were not printed in the *New Discourse*.

Guide to Further Reading

Very little has been written about Hermann Conring in English. He has not attracted much attention from historians in the United Kingdom or the United States, and he is not even mentioned in the *Encyclopedia Britannica* (I checked the on-line version, most recently on 31 March 2002). There is, of course, a large and growing body of books in English on medieval and early modern European history. Many good books have also been written in English about early modern Germany and more particularly about early modern historical and political thought. But whether it is because of national prejudice, the distasteful aspects of German history in the twentieth century, contemporary historiographical fashion, or for some other reason—the simple fact of the matter is that, apart from the Protestant Reformation, the history of early modern Germany, the history of the Holy Roman Empire, and especially the history of early modern German legal and political thought have not nearly received as much scholarly attention in English as they have in German. Yet these are precisely the subjects in which Conring was most interested and to the history of which he made the most important contributions.

That makes it impossible to guide the reader to further reading about Hermann Conring without giving pride of place to German scholarship. Readers of this translation may of course not be able to read German well, or read it at all. I have therefore made a special effort to include writings in English. These will unfortunately not do very much to inform readers about Hermann Conring himself, and they will cast the background to his life and work in a somewhat different light from the light cast by books written in German, illuminating some areas more brightly, leaving others in the dark. But they will introduce readers to the world in which Conring lived, the subjects in which he was interested, and the problems he confronted. Some of them have very good bibliographies and indices. With their help, readers will be able to learn enough for a first approach to Hermann Conring's place in European history. And perhaps their interest will be stimulated to learn more.

The indispensable starting point for information about Conring's life and works is Michael Stolleis, ed., *Hermann Conring, 1606–1681: Beiträge zu Leben und Werk*, Historische Forschungen 23 (Berlin: Duncker & Humblot, 1983). This is a collection of scholarly papers on the most important aspects of Conring's life and thought written by an impressive number of highly regarded experts in German history for a conference at the Herzog August Bibliothek in Wolfenbüttel on the occasion of the three-hundredth anniversary of Conring's death. It approaches Conring from many different angles: biographical, intellectual, his political thought and his political activity, his library, his medical knowledge, his thoughts on history, his career as a professor, his views on theology and law, his relations with diplomats and statesmen in Germany, France, and Sweden, and other subjects besides. It also refers to most of the older literature and contains the most comprehensive and reliable bibliography of Conring's published and unpublished writings. It does not make up for the lack of a good biography. But it does represent the current state of scholarship.

Particularly useful as an introduction to Conring's life and the range of his intellectual pursuits is the catalog of the exhibition that was organized at the Herzog August Bibliothek in Wolfenbüttel on the same occasion by Patricia Herberger and Michael Stolleis, *Hermann Conring, 1606–1681: Ein Gelehrter der Universität Helmstedt* (Wolfenbüttel: Herzog August Bibliothek, 1981). This is handsomely illustrated and full of detailed information, about not only Conring himself, but also his family, friends, and teachers, his income and his estates, the disciplines in which he specialized, the region of Germany in which he lived, the diplomats, statesmen, and princes with whom he corresponded, the University of Helmstedt, and the context of early modern German history more broadly speaking.

Conring's published output was enormous. The bibliography by William Ashford Kelly and Michael Stolleis, "Hermann Conring: Gedruckte Werke, 1627–1751," in *Beiträge*, 535–72, lists more than two hundred ninety separate items. Most of these were printed during his lifetime. But several did not see the light of day until 1730, when they appeared in Johann Wilhelm Goebel's edition of Conring's works, *Viri quondam illustris Hermanni Conringii polyhistoris celeberrimi... Operum tomus I.–VI.* (Brunswick: Meyer, 1730; repr. Aalen: Scientia, 1970–1973), and there is a significant number of writings that were never printed at all. Goebel's edition itself, moreover, is sadly incomplete. It includes only about one hundred fifty of the published works listed by Kelly and Stolleis, just over half the total. Neither its massive size—six large folio volumes and an index volume—nor its designation as *Opera* should mislead readers into thinking that it amounts to anything like a reliable guide to Conring's intellectual life as a whole. Readers will look in vain for his introduction to medicine, his defense of Harvey's theory of the circulation of the blood, his account of the source of heat in the human body, or his attack on Paracelsus. Nor will they find his (unfinished) survey of natural philosophy. And they may never realize that Conring produced not only a sizeable body of writings on assorted theological issues, but also numerous "programs" that he presented to the University of Helmstedt in one or another official capacity over the years. Whoever is interested in Conring's writings on natural philosophy and medicine, his polemics with Catholic writers in the aftermath of the Peace of Westphalia, and many of his minor writings thus has no choice but to track down the original copies published separately in the seventeenth century.

By the early nineteenth century Conring had been consigned to oblivion. Friedrich Karl von Savigny does not so much as mention him in his *Geschichte des römischen Rechts im Mittelalter*, 6 vols. (Heidelberg: Mohr, 1815–1831). He was not remembered again until Otto Stobbe, a noted historian of German law, became rector of the University of Breslau in 1869. Living in the days of German national unification, Stobbe devoted his inaugural address to impressing upon his audience the role Conring had played as a historian of German law. Published under the title *Hermann Conring, der Begründer der deutschen Rechtsgeschichte* (Berlin: W. Hertz, 1870), this was the first work to draw significant scholarly attention to Conring. It placed Conring in a decidedly national context and was followed by a series of studies, often dissertations, on particular aspects of Conring's life and works that appeared in the late nineteenth and early twentieth centuries. Thus Nathan Goldschlag, *Beiträge zur politischen und publizistischen Thätigkeit Herman* [sic] *Conrings* (Berlin: A. Winser, 1884), and Paul Felberg, *Conrings Anteil am politischen Leben seiner Zeit* (Trier: Paulinus, 1931), focused on Conring's role as an adviser to diplomats and statesmen in Germany, Sweden, and France. Robert Knoll, *Hermann Conring als Historiker* (Rostock: Universitäts-Buchdruckerei von Adler's Erben, 1889), and Karl Kossert, *Hermann Conrings rechtsgeschichtliches Verdienst* (Köln: Orthen, 1939), reviewed Conring's historical investigations. Reinold Zehrfeld, *Hermann Conrings (1606–1681) Staatenkunde: Ihre Bedeutung für die Geschichte der Statistik unter besonderer Berücksichtigung der Conringschen Bevölkerungslehre* (Berlin: W. de Gruyter, 1926), investigated Conring's contribution to the development of statistics, as did Ferdinand Felsing, *Die Statistik als Methode der politischen Ökonomie im 17. und 18. Jahrhundert* (Borna-Leipzig: R. Noske, 1930). Specialized studies such as these—all listed in the *Beiträge* edited by Stolleis— are still worth reading for details. But by now they have been superseded in many ways and they never did amount to a coherent intellectual picture.

The best biography is the old work by Ernst von Moeller, *Hermann Conring, der Vorkämpfer des deutschen Rechts, 1606–1681*, Quellen und Darstellungen zur Geschichte Niedersachsens 31 (Hannover: E. Geibel, 1915). Moeller is particularly good on Conring's early life, in part because he was able to draw on sources that have been lost since then. But he paid little attention to Conring's voluminous correspondence and limited himself on many pages of his book to lengthy summaries of Conring's best-known writings. Other than Moeller's book, there are several brief sketches usually repeating much of the same information. Especially interesting is the above-mentioned inaugural address by Otto Stobbe. Also worth mentioning are a much-cited essay by Erik Wolf, "Hermann Conring," in *Grosse Rechtsdenker der deutschen Geistesgeschichte*, 4th ed. (Tübingen: Mohr,

1963), 220–52; the summation by Michael Stolleis, "Die Einheit der Wissenschaften: Hermann Conring, 1606–1681," in *Beiträge*, 11–31, and a piece by Dietmar Willoweit, "Hermann Conring," in *Staatsdenker in der frühen Neuzeit*, ed. Michael Stolleis, 3rd ed. (Munich: C. H. Beck, 1995), 129–47. In English, the best available sketches are by Hanns Gross, *Empire and Sovereignty: A History of the Public Law Literature in the Holy Roman Empire, 1599–1804* (Chicago: University of Chicago Press, 1975), 255–92, and William A. Kelly, *Hermann Conring (1606–1681): A Study in Versatility* (East Linton: The Cat's Whiskers Press, 1993). The latter is a revised version of the second chapter of a thesis submitted by Kelly to the Library Association in Scotland in 1982 and apparently published by himself.

Since the publication of the *Beiträge zu Leben und Werk* in 1983, some further works specifically devoted to Hermann Conring have appeared in print. Above all there is now a German translation of Conring's single most famous piece of writing, the *De origine iuris Germanici commentarius historicus* of 1643, under the title *Der Ursprung des deutschen Rechts*, ed. Michael Stolleis, trans. Ilse Hoffmann-Meckenstock (Frankfurt: Insel Verlag, 1994), with an excellent introduction by Stolleis to Conring's significance for the history of German law. Horst Dreitzel has published an article on "Aristoteles' Politik im Denken Hermann Conrings," in *Categorie del reale e storiographia: Aspetti di continuità e trasformazione nell' Europa moderna*, ed. F. Fagiani and G. Valera (Milano: Franco Angeli, 1986), 33–59. Arno Seifert included a penetrating analysis of Conring's recasting of German imperial history in his *Der Rückzug der biblischen Prophetie von der neueren Geschichte* (Cologne: Böhlau, 1990), 165–86. Heiko Droste, "Hermann Conring und Schweden: Eine vielschichtige Beziehung," *Ius Commune* 26 (1999): 337–62, is the best piece to have been written about Conring's relations to Sweden since Nathan Goldschlag's dissertation of 1884.[1] And I have published several articles on the *New Discourse* and Conring's historical thought more broadly speaking: "Conring on History," in *Supplementum Festivum: Studies in Honor of Paul Oskar Kristeller*, ed. James Hankins, John Monfasani, and Frederick Purnell, MRTS 49 (Binghamton: Medieval and Renaissance Texts and Studies, 1987), 563–87; "A Question of Right: Hermann Conring's *New Discourse on the Roman-German Emperor*," *Sixteenth Century Journal* 28 (1997): 739–58; and "Author and Authenticity in Conring's *New Discourse on the Roman-German Emperor*: A Seventeenth-Century Case Study," *Renaissance Quarterly* 54 (2001): 188–220. I have also made Conring the central character in a book entitled *The Limits of History* (Chicago: University of Chicago Press, 2004). But that book, as its title is meant to clarify,

---

[1] I am grateful to Erik Thomson for having drawn my attention to this piece.

is devoted to an investigation of historical knowledge as such. It does not meet the need for a comprehensive study of Hermann Conring's life and works. His correspondence, his medical and scientific writings, his confessional polemics, his account of the history of the Roman empire after the Peace of Westphalia, and his analysis of the conflict between the city and archbishop of Cologne (to mention only the most obvious omissions) are all still far from having received the scholarly examination they deserve.

Readers who would like to know more about Conring's place in the history of early modern political thought will do well to start with Franz Wieacker, *History of Private Law in Europe with Particular Reference to Germany*, trans. Tony Weir (Oxford: Clarendon Press, 1995). This is a recent English translation of Franz Wieacker, *Privatrechtsgeschichte der Neuzeit: Unter besonderer Berücksichtigung der deutschen Entwicklung*, 2nd ed. (Göttingen: Vandenhoeck & Ruprecht, 1967), originally published in 1952, and bearing a title unfortunately well designed to conceal its originality, breadth, and fundamental importance. Because it deals with the whole sweep of German legal history, from the Middle Ages to the twentieth century, and does so from a broadly European perspective on the fundamental conditions of European intellectual life as a whole, few other books furnish a more appropriate frame of reference for judging Conring's significance.

Those who read German may also turn to Michael Stolleis, *Reichspublizistik und Policeywissenschaft, 1600–1800*, vol. 1 of *Geschichte des öffentlichen Rechts in Deutschland* (Munich: C. H. Beck, 1988). Though this title, too, may lead the unwary into thinking that Stolleis deals only with law, in fact he offers as good an account of early modern German political thought as will be found anywhere. Given the famously close relationship between questions of law and questions of politics in German history, "public law" was the most natural heading under which German writers chose to deal with questions of politics in the early modern period. Expanding on the foundation laid by Wieacker, Stolleis traces the intellectual and historical context in which this literature developed, describes its explosive growth after about 1600, offers thumbnail sketches of all the major and many of the minor figures involved, and includes comprehensive bibliographical information. Readers who would prefer to inform themselves quickly about a few important authors and issues may consult Michael Stolleis, ed., *Staatsdenker in der frühen Neuzeit*, 3rd ed. (Munich: C. H. Beck, 1995), which consists of short biographies of some particularly well-known writers, and Michael Stolleis, *Staat und Staatsräson in der frühen Neuzeit: Studien zur Geschichte des öffentlichen Rechts* (Frankfurt am Main: Suhrkamp, 1990), which addresses conceptual and historical issues of special importance to the history of early modern political thought.

Four other books will help to round out the picture. Horst Dreitzel, *Protestantischer Absolutismus und absoluter Staat: Die "Politica" des Henning Arnisaeus, ca. 1575–1636* (Wiesbaden: R. Steiner, 1970) remains the most substantial account of political thought in seventeenth-century Germany to focus on the forms of Aristotelianism to which German Protestant thinkers like Conring were specially devoted. Gross, *Empire and Sovereignty* covers some of the same territory as Michael Stolleis, but with a more explicit focus on the question of sovereignty. Leonard Krieger, *The German Idea of Freedom: History of a Political Tradition from the Reformation to 1871* (Chicago: University of Chicago Press, 1957) may still be read with profit as a particularly influential attempt to characterize the whole trajectory of early modern German political thought as divergent from that of the West. And particularly useful for understanding the ways in which Germans began to distance themselves from "the Middle Ages" is Uwe Neddermeyer, *Das Mittelalter in der deutschen Historiographie vom 15. bis zum 18. Jahrhundert: Geschichtsgliederung und Epochenverständnis in der frühen Neuzeit* (Cologne: Böhlau, 1988).

Concerning the history of the Holy Roman Empire, one of the most informative books for readers of English is a collection edited by Gerald Strauss under the title *Pre-Reformation Germany* (New York: Harper, 1972). This contains translations of essays by German historians such as Karl Bader, Heinrich Heimpel, Fritz Hartung, Georg Dahm, Wolfgang Kunkel, Paul Joachimsen, Friedrich Lütge, and Bernd Moeller on some of the most important features of early modern German history. It is, for all intents and purposes, the best place for English readers to inform themselves about the views on early modern German history held by some of the most influential German historians of the twentieth century. Since it highlights constitutional and legal history, it is a particularly useful source of information about the historical context by which Conring's interests were shaped. Two other collections of essays in English will bring readers face to face with some of the central issues in more recent debates about the Holy Roman Empire by German, English, and American historians: James A. Vann and Steven W. Rowan, eds., *The Old Reich: Essays on German Political Institutions, 1495–1806* (Bruxelles: Librairie Encyclopédique, 1974); and John Boyer and Julius Kirshner, eds., *Politics and Society in the Holy Roman Empire, 1500–1806* (Chicago: University of Chicago Press, 1986).

Among more leisurely histories on the grand scale and written by individual historians, the old work by Moriz Ritter, *Deutsche Geschichte im Zeitalter der Gegenreformation und des Dreissigjährigen Krieges, 1555–1648*, 3 vols. (Stuttgart: Cotta, 1889–1908) still makes for as readable and detailed a general history as any that has been written since then. More recent studies have been published by Heinz Angermeier, *Die Reichsreform 1410–1555: Die Staatsproblematik in Deutschland zwischen Mittelalter und Gegenwart* (Munich: C. H. Beck, 1984), who focuses on the empire's response to the crisis of the late Middle Ages; Heinrich Lutz, *Das Ringen um deutsche Einheit und kirchliche Erneuerung: Von Maximilian I. bis zum Westfälischen Frieden, 1490 bis 1648* (Berlin: Propyläen Verlag, 1983), who reviews the fate of the empire during the age of religious reformation and war; and Fritz Dickmann, *Der Westfälische Frieden*, ed. Konrad Repgen, 4th ed. (Münster: Aschendorff, 1977), who furnishes indispensable information about the events of Conring's own times. Karl Otmar Freiherr von Aretin, *Das Alte Reich, 1648–1806*, 3 vols. (Stuttgart: Klett-Cotta, 1993–1997), deserves special mention as a unique and exceptionally well-informed attempt to write the history, neither of Germany nor of the German territories, but of the empire as such. In English, Hajo Holborn, *A History of Modern Germany*, 3 vols. (New York: Knopf, 1959–1969), has not been surpassed, although there are now several more recent works treating more narrowly defined periods, as for example Michael Hughes, *Early Modern Germany, 1477–1806* (Philadelphia: University of Pennsylvania Press, 1992); John Gagliardo, *Germany Under the Old Regime, 1600–1792* (London: Longman, 1991); and Ronald G. Asch, *The Thirty Years War: The Holy Roman Empire and Europe, 1618–48* (New York: St. Martin's Press, 1997).

For the European background to Conring's ideas about politics, readers of English are in the fortunate position of being able to draw on a growing array of up-to-date surveys and handbooks. For the Middle Ages, to whose history many of Conring's investigations were devoted, the best starting points are two short introductions by Joseph Canning, *A History of Medieval Political Thought, 300–1450* (London: Routledge, 1996), and Antony Black, *Political Thought in Europe, 1250–1450* (Cambridge: Cambridge University Press, 1992), or the comprehensive handbook by J. H. Burns, ed., *Cambridge History of Medieval Political Thought, c. 350 – c. 1450* (Cambridge: Cambridge University Press, 1988). For the early modern period the best places to begin are the deservedly famous survey by Quentin Skinner, *The Foundations of Modern Political Thought*, 2 vols. (Cambridge: Cambridge University Press, 1978); the more recent survey by Richard Tuck, *Philosophy and Government, 1572–1651* (Cambridge: Cambridge University Press, 1992); and the handbook by J. H. Burns and Mark Goldie, eds., *Cambridge History of Political Thought, 1450–1700* (Cambridge: Cambridge University Press, 1991). Readers who would like more information on parallels and precursors to Conring's thinking about the relationship between politics and history in France and England should turn to Julian H. Franklin, *Jean Bodin and the Sixteenth-Century Revolution in the Methodology of Law and History* (New York: Columbia University Press, 1963); Donald R. Kelley, *Foundations of Modern Historical Scholarship: Language, Law, and History in the French Renaissance* (New York: Columbia University Press, 1970); and J. G. A. Pocock, *The Ancient Constitution and the Feudal Law: A Study of English Historical Thought in the Seventeenth Century*, rev. ed. (Cambridge: Cambridge University Press, 1987). For the new periodization of history brought about by humanism, readers can hardly do better than to turn to the classic essay by Theodor E. Mommsen, "Petrarch's Conception of the 'Dark Ages'," in idem, *Medieval and Renaissance Studies*, ed. Eugene F. Rice (Ithaca:

Cornell University Press, 1959), 106–29, first published in *Speculum* 17 (1942): 226–42.

For more information about what one may call the western imperial tradition, readers might begin by consulting the standard survey by Robert Folz, *The Concept of Empire in Western Europe from the Fifth to the Fourteenth Century*, trans. Sheila Ann Ogilvie (London: Edward Arnold, 1969). More important for early modern conceptions of empire in Europe are the influential study by Frances Yates, *Astraea: The Imperial Theme in the Sixteenth Century* (London and Boston: Routledge & K. Paul, 1975); the study of universal monarchy by Franz Bosbach, *Monarchia universalis: Ein politischer Leitbegriff der frühen Neuzeit* (Göttingen: Vandenhoeck & Ruprecht, 1988); and the works of John M. Headley, especially *The Emperor and His Chancellor: A Study of the Imperial Chancellery under Gattinara* (Cambridge: Cambridge University Press, 1983), and the articles collected in *Church, Empire, and World: The Quest for Universal Order, 1520–1640* (Aldershot: Ashgate, 1997). Imperial ideas on the cusp between Europe and other continents have drawn the attention of Anthony Pagden, *Lords of all the World: Ideologies of Empire in Spain, Britain and France c. 1500–c. 1800* (New Haven: Yale University Press, 1995), and James Muldoon, *Empire and Order: The Concept of Empire, 800–1800* (New York: St. Martin's Press, 1999). For a wide-ranging collection of essays, see David Armitage, ed., *Theories of Empire, 1450–1800* (Aldershot: Ashgate, 1998).

The problematic of the term "state," of course, is huge. Nothing more than a sampling of the range of different approaches—old and new, for and against—taken by historians of political thought, institutional historians, anthropologists, philosophers, and political scientists can be offered here. The following introductory pieces may prove particularly useful for obtaining conceptual and definitional clarity about the basic issues: H. C. Dowdal, "The Word 'State'," *Law Quarterly Review* 39 (1923): 98–125; Quentin Skinner, "The State," in *Political Innovation and Conceptual Change*, ed. Terence Ball, James Farr, and Russell Hanson (Cambridge: Cambridge University Press, 1989), 90–131; and Reinhart Koselleck, Werner Conze, Görg Haverkate, Diethelm Klippel, and Hans Boldt, "Staat und Souveränität," in *Geschichtliche Grundbegriffe: Historisches Lexikon zur politisch-sozialen Sprache in Deutschland*, ed. Otto Brunner, Werner Conze, and Reinhart Koselleck (Stuttgart: Klett, 1972–1992), 6:1–154. For broad historically-oriented surveys of theories of state and sovereignty, see Andrew Vincent, *Theories of the State* (Oxford: Blackwell, 1987), and Francis H. Hinsley, *Sovereignty*, 2nd ed. (Cambridge: Cambridge University Press, 1986).

For a few influential studies that are strikingly different in their methods, assumptions, and conclusions, see Friedrich Meinecke, *Machiavellism: The Doctrine of Raison d'Etat and its Place in Modern History*, trans. Douglas Scott (New Haven: Yale University Press, 1957); Ernst Cassirer, *The Myth of the State* (New Haven: Yale University Press, 1946); Ronald Cohen and Elman R. Service, eds., *Origins of the State: The Anthropology of Political Evolution* (Philadelphia: Institute for the Study of Human Issues, 1978); Otto Brunner, *Land and Lordship: Structures of Governance in Medieval Austria*, trans. with an introduction by Howard Kaminsky and James Van Horn Melton (Philadelphia: University of Pennsylvania Press, 1992); Joseph R. Strayer, *On the Medieval Origins of the Modern State* (Princeton: Princeton University Press, 1970); Perry Anderson, *Lineages of the Absolutist State* (London: N.L.B., 1974); and Janet Coleman, *Against the State: Studies in Sedition and Rebellion* (Harmondsworth: Penguin Books, 1995).

Debates about the meaning of the term "republic" have recently become similarly vexed, though they are perhaps not as deeply lodged in historical consciousness. See for example Wolfgang Mager, "Republik," in *Geschichtliche Grundbegriffe*, 5:549–651; Helmut G. Koenigsberger, ed., *Republiken und Republikanismus im Europa der frühen Neuzeit* (Munich: Oldenbourg, 1988); Gerhard Dilcher, ed., *Res publica: Bürgerschaft in Stadt und Staat* (Berlin: Duncker & Humblot, 1988); Gisela Bock, Quentin Skinner, and Maurizio Viroli, eds., *Machiavelli and Republicanism* (Cambridge: Cambridge University Press, 1990); Anthony Pagden, ed., *The Languages of Political Theory in Early-Modern Europe* (Cambridge: Cambridge University Press, 1987); J. G. A. Pocock, Gordon J. Schochet, and Lois G. Schwoerer, eds., *The Varieties of British Political Thought, 1500–1800* (Cambridge: Cambridge University Press, 1994); J. G. A. Pocock, "States, Republics, and Empires: The American Founding in Early-Modern Perspective," in *Conceptual Change and the Constitution*, ed. Terence Ball and J. G. A. Pocock (Lawrence: University Press of Kansas, 1988), 55–77; and Michael P. Zuckert, *Natural Rights and the New Republicanism* (Princeton: Princeton University Press, 1994).

Finally, since Conring was so very much concerned to distinguish medieval German history from the history of the Roman empire, readers may wish to know how medieval German history is viewed by experts today. The best German scholarship on the early medieval period is embodied in Johannes Fried's brilliant book *Der Weg in die Geschichte: Die Ursprünge Deutschlands bis 1024* (Berlin: Propyläen Verlag, 1994). The later phases of medieval German history are treated in the same series by Hagen Keller, *Zwischen regionaler Begrenzung und universalem Horizont: Deutschland im Imperium der Salier und Staufer, 1024 bis 1250* (Berlin: Propyläen Verlag, 1986), and Peter Moraw, *Von offener Verfassung zu gestalteter Verdichtung: Das Reich im späten Mittelalter, 1250 bis 1490* (Berlin: Propyläen Verlag, 1985). For more technical information and copious references to sources and older scholarship, Herbert Grundmann, ed., *Gebhardt: Handbuch der deutschen Geschichte*, 9th ed., 4 vols. (Stuttgart: Union Verlag, 1970–1976), is still very useful, but a new edition is in progress.

Among books in English, Geoffrey Barraclough, *The Origins of Modern Germany*, rev. ed. (Oxford: Blackwell, 1947), is in spite of its age and idiosyncratic point of view still a lively single-volume treatment of German history from the

Middle Ages to the twentieth century. Even older and still grander in its way is James Bryce, *The Holy Roman Empire*, rev. ed. (New York: Schocken Books, 1961; first published 1864). For accounts of German history that are less sweeping, but also more up-to-date in terms of scholarship, see Malcolm Todd, *The Early Germans* (Oxford: Blackwell, 1992) for the earliest times; Timothy Reuter, *Germany in the Early Middle Ages, 800–1056* (London: Longman, 1991); Horst Fuhrmann, *Germany in the High Middle Ages, c. 1050–1200*, trans. Timothy Reuter (Cambridge: Cambridge University Press, 1986); Alfred Haverkamp, *Medieval Germany, 1056–1273*, trans. Helga Braun and Richard Mortimer, 2nd ed. (Oxford: Oxford University Press, 1992); Joachim Leuschner, *Germany in the Late Middle Ages*, trans. Sabine MacCormack (Amsterdam: North-Holland Pub. Co., 1980); and F. R. H. Du Boulay, *Germany in the Later Middle Ages* (New York: St. Martin's Press, 1983).

WORKS CITED IN THE *NEW DISCOURSE*

The following list is limited to works cited in the *New Discourse* itself. I have made no effort to identify the particular editions on which Conring relied, but I have verified that the editions listed below do in fact contain the passages to which Conring refers. Where I was aware of recent critical editions or English translations, I have added information about those, even in cases in which I used an early modern printed edition as my main point of reference.

Adalbert. "Adalberti continuatio Reginonis. Adalberts Fortsetzung der Chronik Reginos." In *Quellen zur Geschichte der Sächsischen Kaiserzeit*, ed. and trans. Albert Bauer and Reinhold Rau, 185–231. Ausgewählte Quellen zur deutschen Geschichte des Mittelalters 8. Darmstadt: Wissenschaftliche Buchgesellschaft, 1977. See also *PL* 132:151–174.

Ado of Vienne. "Ex Adonis archiepiscopi Viennensis Chronico." In *Scriptores*, ed. Georg Heinrich Pertz, 2:315–26. Monumenta Germaniae Historica. Hannover: Hahn, 1829. See also *PL* 123:23–138.

Anastasius Bibliothecarius. *Historia de vitis Romanorum pontificum a b. Petro apostolo usque ad Nicolaum I. nunquam hactenus typis excusa. Deinde vita Hadriani II. et Stephani VI. auctore Guilielmo bibliothecario.* Moguntiae: In typographeio Ioannis Albini, 1602. See also Louis Duchesne, ed. *Le Liber pontificalis: Texte, introduction et commentaire.* 2nd ed. 3 vols. Bibliothèque des Ecoles françaises d'Athènes et de Rome, 2nd ser., 3. Paris: E. de Boccard, 1955–1957. Also *PL* 127–128. Cf. *The Book of Pontiffs (Liber pontificalis): The Ancient Biographies of the First Ninety Roman Bishops to A.D. 715*, trans. Raymond Davis. Liverpool: Liverpool University Press, 1989; *Lives of the Eighth-Century Popes: Liber Pontificalis, 715–817 A.D.*, trans. Raymond Davis. Liverpool: Liverpool University Press, 1992.

Annales regum Francorum, Pippini, Caroli Magni et Lodovici, ab anno 741. usque ad annum 829. Coloniae: Ioannes Birckmannus, 1562. See also "Annales Regni Francorum. Die Reichsannalen," in *Quellen zur Karolingischen Reichsgeschichte. Erster Teil*, ed. and trans. Reinhold Rau, 9–155. Ausgewählte Quellen zur deutschen Geschichte des Mittelalters 5. Darmstadt: Wissenschaftliche Buchgesellschaft, 1977. Also *PL* 104:367–508. Cf. *Carolingian Chronicles: Royal Frankish Annals and Nithard's Histories*, trans. Bernhard Walter Scholz, 35–125. Ann Arbor: University of Michigan Press, 1970.

Baronio, Cesare. *Annales ecclesiastici*. 38 vols. Lucae: Typis L. Venturini, 1738–1759.

Bartolus of Sassoferrato. *Opera*. 12 vols. Venetiis: Apud Iuntas, 1570–1571.

Bauer, Albert, and Reinhold Rau, eds. and trans. *Quellen zur Geschichte der Sächsischen Kaiserzeit*. Ausgewählte Quellen zur deutschen Geschichte des Mittelalters 8. Darmstadt: Wissenschaftliche Buchgesellschaft, 1977.

Bellarmino, Roberto Francesco Romolo. *De translatione imperii Romani a Graecis ad Francos, adversus Matthiam Flaccium Illyricum libri tres*. Antverpiae: Ex officina C. Plantini, 1589.

The Bible.

Biondo, Flavio. *Historiarum ab inclinatione Romanorum imperii libri xxxi*. Basileae: Froben, 1559. See also *Le decadi: Historiarum ab inclinatione Romanorum decades libri XXXI*, trans. Achille Crespi. Castrocaro Terme: Comune di Forlì, 1963.

Bodin, Jean. *Les six livres de la république*. Ed. Christiane Frémont, Marie-Dominique Couzinet, and Henri Rochais. 6 vols. Corpus des oeuvres de philosophie en langue française. Paris: Fayard, 1986. Cf. Jean Bodin, *The Six Books of a Commonweale*, ed. Kenneth D. McRae, trans. Richard Knolles. Cambridge, MA: Harvard University Press, 1962.

Canisius, Henricus, ed. *Chronicon Victoris episcopi Tunnunensis. Chronicon Joannis Biclarensis... Legatio Luitprandi episcopi Cremonensis ad Nicephorum Phocam*. Ingolstadii: Officina typographica Ederiana, apud Andream Angermarium, 1600.

Chronicon Salernitanum: see Westerbergh, Ulla.

Corpus Iuris: see Justinian.

Continuator of Regino: *see* Adalbert.

Davis, Raymond, ed. *The Book of Pontiffs (Liber pontificalis): The Ancient Biographies of the First Ninety Roman Bishops to A.D. 715*. Trans. with an introduction by Raymond Davis. Translated Texts for Historians: Latin series, 5. Liverpool: Liverpool University Press, 1989.

— ed. *Lives of the Eighth-Century Popes: Liber Pontificalis, 715–817 A.D.* Trans. Raymond Davis. Translated Texts for Historians, 13. Liverpool: Liverpool University Press, 1992.

Dionysius of Halicarnassus. *The Roman Antiquities of Dionysius of Halicarnassus.* Trans. Earnest Cary. 7 vols. Loeb Classical Library. Cambridge, MA: Harvard University Press, 1937–1950.

Duchesne, André. *Historiae Francorum scriptores coaetanei ab ipsius gentis origine.* 5 vols. Parisiis: Sumptibus S. Cramoisy, 1636–1649.

Duchesne, Louis, ed. *Le Liber pontificalis: Texte, introduction et commentaire.* 2nd ed. 3 vols. Bibliothèque des Ecoles françaises d'Athènes et de Rome, 2nd ser., 3. Paris: E. de Boccard, 1955–1957.

Einhard. "Vita Karoli Magni." In *Quellen zur Karolingischen Reichsgeschichte. Erster Teil*, ed. and trans. Rau, 163–211. See also *PL* 97:25–62. Cf. "The Life of Charlemagne," in *Two Lives of Charlemagne*, trans. Lewis Thorpe, 46–90. Harmondsworth: Penguin, 1969.

Frankish Annals: see *Annales regum Francorum*.

Freher, Marquard, ed. *Constantini magni imperatoris donatio Sylvestro papae Romano inscripta, non ut a Gratiano truncatim, sed integre edita. Cum versione Graeca duplici, Theodori Balsamonis, patriarchae Antiocheni, et Matthaei Blastaris, iurisconsulti Graeci. Item Otthonis III. imperatoris donatio Sylvestro II. papae facta, in qua de fide et auctore Constantinianae testimonium. Commentariis amplissimis illustrata.* Heidelberg: Typis G. Voegelini, 1610. The commentaries in this volume have also been attributed to Isaac Casaubon.

Glaber, Raoul. *Rodulfi Glabri Historiarum libri quinque. The Five Books of the Histories.* Ed. and trans. John France. Oxford Medieval Texts. Oxford: Oxford University Press, 1989. See also *PL* 142:611–698.

Godefridus Viterbiensis. "Pantheon." In idem, *Opera*, ed. Georg Waitz, 107–307. Monumenta Germaniae Historica, Scriptores 22. Hannover: Hahn, 1872. See also *PL* 198:875–1044.

Gratian. *Decretum Magistri Gratiani.* Ed. E. Friedberg. Corpus Iuris Canonici 1. Leipzig: B. Tauchnitz, 1879. See also *PL* 187.

Grotius, Hugo. *Liber de antiquitate reipublicae Batavicae.* Lugduni Batavorum: Ex officina Plantiniana Raphelengij, 1610.

— *Apologeticus eorum qui Hollandiae Westfrisiaeque et vicinis quibusdam nationibus ex legibus praefuerunt ante mutationem quae evenit anno MDCXVIII.* Parisiis: Sumptibus Nicolai Buon, 1622.

— *De iure belli ac pacis libri tres.* Ed. James Brown Scott. Trans. Francis W. Kelsey. 2 vols. Washington, DC: Carnegie Institution, 1913–1925.

Hincmar of Reims. "Ad Ludovicum Balbum regem: Novi regis instructio ad rectam regni administrationem." In *Hincmari archiepiscopi Remensis opera duos in tomos digesta*, ed. Jacques Sirmond, 2:179–84. Lutetiae Parisiorum: Sumtibus Sebastiani Cramoisy, Architypographi Regis & Reginae regentis, et Gabrielis Cramoisy, 1645. See also *PL* 125:983–990.

"Historia Erphesfordensis anonymi scriptoris de landgraviis Thuringiae." In *Illustrium veterum scriptorum, qui rerum a Germanis per multas aetates gestarum historias vel annales posteris reliquerunt, tomus unus*, ed. Johannes Pistorius, 1: 908–60. Francofurti: Impensis C. Marnii haeredum, I. & A. Marnii, 1583.

Isocrates. Trans. George Norlin and Larue van Hook. 3 vols. Loeb Classical Library. London: Heinemann, 1928–1945.

Jordanes. *De origine actibusque Getarum.* Ed. Francesco Giunta and Antonino Grillone. Fonti per la storia d'Italia 117, ed. Istituto storico italiano per il Medio Evo. Roma: Nella sede dell' istituto Palazzo Borromini, 1991. See also *PL* 69:1251–1296. Cf. *The Gothic History of Jordanes in English Version*, trans. Charles Christopher Mierow. Princeton: Princeton University Press, 1915.

Justinian. *Corpus iuris civilis in quatuor partes distinctum.* Ed. Dionysius Gothofredus. 2 vols. Francofurti ad Moenum: Sumptibus Societatis, typis B. C. Wustii sen., 1688. See also *Corpus Iuris Civilis*, ed. Theodor Mommsen, Paul Krüger, Rudolf Schoell, et al. 3 vols. Berlin: Weidmann, 1872–1895. Cf. *The Digest of Justinian*, trans. Alan Watson. 4 vols. Philadelphia: University of Pennsylvania Press, 1985.

Krantz, Albert. *Saxonia et metropolis.* Rev. ed. Coloniae: Apud Gerwinum Calenium & haeredes Quentelios, 1574.

— *Ecclesiastica historia, siue Metropolis.* Rev. ed. Francofurti ad Moenum: Ex officina typographica And. Wecheli, 1576.

Leo Marsicanus, Cardinal Bishop of Ostia. *Chronicon antiquum sacri monasterii Cassinensis.* Neapoli: Ex Typ. T. Longhi, 1616. See also *Die Chronik von Montecassino*, ed. Hartmut Hoffmann. Monumenta Germaniae Historica, Scriptores 34. Hannover: Hahn, 1980; *Cronaca di Montecassino* (III 26–33), ed. F. Aceto and V. Lucherini. Milan: Jaca, 2001; and *PL* 173:479–978.

Liber pontificalis: see Anastasius Bibliothecarius; Davis; Duchesne.

Lipsius, Justus. *Admiranda, siue de magnitudine Romana libri quattuor.* 2nd ed. Antverpiae: Ex officina Plantiniana, apud Ioannem Moretum, 1599.

Liudprand of Cremona. "Legatio ad imperatorem Constantinopolitanum Nicephorum Phocam." In *Quellen zur Geschichte der Sächsischen Kaiserzeit*, ed. and trans. Bauer and Rau, 524–89. See also *PL* 136:909–938. Cf. *The Works of Liudprand of Cremona*, trans. F. A. Wright, 233–77. New York: E. P. Dutton, 1930.

— "Liber de Ottone rege." In *Quellen zur Geschichte der Sächsischen Kaiserzeit*, ed. and trans. Bauer and Rau, 496–523. See also André Duchesne. *Historiae Francorum scriptores*. 5 vols. 3:627–34. Paris: Sumptibus S. Cramoisy, 1636–1649. Also *PL* 136:898–910. Cf. *The Works of Liudprand of Cremona*, trans. Wright, 213–32.

— "Antapodosis." In *Quellen zur Geschichte der Sächsischen Kaiserzeit*, ed. and trans. Bauer and Rau, 244–495. See also Duchesne, *Historiae Francorum scriptores*, 3:562–634, and *PL* 136:787–898. Cf. *The Works of Liudprand of Cremona*, trans. Wright, 25–212.

Niem, Dietrich of. "Privilegia aut iura imperii circa investituras episcopatuum et abbatiarum restituta a papis imperatoribus Romanis." In Simon Schard, *De iurisdictione, autoritate, et praeeminentia imperiali ac potestate ecclesiastica*, 785–859. Basileae: Oporinus, 1566.

Nithard. "Historiarum libri IIII. Vier Bücher Geschichten." In *Quellen zur Karolingischen Reichsgeschichte. Erster Teil*, ed. and trans. Rau, 385–461. See also *PL* 116:45–76. Cf. "Nithard's Histories," in *Carolingian Chronicles: Royal Frankish Annals and Nithard's Histories*, trans. Scholz, 127–74.

Otto of Freising. *Chronica sive historia de duabus civitatibus. Chronik oder die Geschichte der zwei Staaten.* Ed. Walther Lammers. Trans. Adolf Schmidt. Ausgewählte Quellen zur deutschen Geschichte des Mittelalters 16. Darmstadt: Wissenschaftliche Buchgesellschaft, 1972. Cf. *The Two Cities: A Chronicle of Universal History to the Year 1146 A.D.*, trans. Charles Christopher Mierow. New York: Columbia University Press, 1928.

Otto of Freising and Rahewin. *Gesta Frederici seu rectius Cronica. Die Taten Friedrichs oder richtiger Cronica.* Ed. Franz-Josef Schmale. Trans. Adolf Schmidt. Ausgewählte Quellen zur deutschen Geschichte des Mittelalters 17. Darmstadt: Wissenschaftliche Buchgesellschaft, 1965. Cf. *The Deeds of Frederick Barbarossa*, trans. Charles Christopher Mierow and Richard Emery. New York: Columbia University Press, 1953.

Panvinio, Onofrio. *Reipublicae Romanae commentariorum libri tres*. Venetiis: Ex officina Erasmiana apud V. Valgrisium, 1558.

Paulus Diaconus. "Historia Langobardorum." In *Scriptores rerum Langobardicarum et Italicarum saec. VI–IX*, ed. L. Bethmann and G. Waitz, 12–219. Monumenta

Germaniae Historica. Hannover: Hahn, 1878. See also *PL* 95:433–672. Cf. *History of the Langobards*, trans. William Dudley Foulke. New York: Longmans, 1907.

Petronius. Trans. Michael Heseltine, rev. E. H. Warmington. Loeb Classical Library. Cambridge, MA: Harvard University Press, 1987.

Pistorius, Johannes. *Illustrium veterum scriptorum, qui rerum a Germanis per multas aetates gestarum historias vel annales posteris reliquerunt, tomus unus*. 2 vols. Francofurti: Impensis C. Marnii haeredum, I. & A. Marnii, 1583–1584.

Pithou, Pierre. *Annalium et historiae Francorum ab anno Christi DCCCCXC. scriptores coaetanei XII*. Francofurti: Apud Andreae Wecheli heredes, Claudium Marnium, & Ioann. Aubrium, 1594.

Platina, Bartolomeo. *De vitis pontificum Romanorum, a D. N. Iesu Christo usque ad Paulum II. Venetum papam*. Coloniae Agrippinae: Ex officina Choliniana, 1626. See also *Liber de vita Christi ac omnium pontificum*, ed. G. Gaida. Rerum Italicarum Scriptores 3.1. Città di Castello: Lapi, 1913–1932. Cf. *The Lives of the Popes from the Time of Our Saviour Jesus Christ to the Death of Paul II.*, ed. William Benham, trans. Paul Rycaut. 2 vols. The Ancient and Modern Library of Theological Literature. London: Griffith, Farran, Okeden & Welsh, 1888.

Plinius Secundus, C. *Natural History*. Trans. H. Rackham and W. H. S. Jones. 10 vols. Loeb Classical Library. Cambridge, MA: Harvard University Press, 1938–1963.

Poeta Saxo. "Annalium de gestis Caroli Magni imperatoris libri quinque." In *Poetae Latini Aevi Carolini*, ed. Paulus de Winterfeld, 4:1–71. Monumenta Germaniae Historica. Berlin: Weidmann, 1899. See also *PL* 99:683–736. Cf. *The Saxon Poet's Life of Charles the Great*, trans. Mary E. McKinney. New York: Pageant Press, 1956.

Puteanus, Erycius. *Historiae insubricae libri vi*. Oxonii: G. Turner, 1634.

Rahewin: *see* Otto of Freising.

Rau, Reinhold, ed. and trans. *Quellen zur Karolingischen Reichsgeschichte. Erster Teil*. Ausgewählte Quellen zur deutschen Geschichte des Mittelalters 5. Darmstadt: Wissenschaftliche Buchgesellschaft, 1977.

Scaliger, Joseph Justus. *Isagogicorum chronologiae canonum libri tres*. In idem, *Thesaurus temporum*, separately paginated. Lugduni Batavorum: Excudebat Thomas Basson, 1606.

Schard, Simon. *De iurisdictione, autoritate, et praeeminentia imperiali ac potestate ecclesiastica deque iuribus regni et imperii, variorum authorum qui ante haec tempora vixerunt scripta, collecta et redacta in unum.* Basileae: Oporinus, 1566.

Scholz, Bernhard Walter, with Barbara Rogers, trans. *Carolingian Chronicles: Royal Frankish Annals and Nithard's Histories.* Ann Arbor: University of Michigan Press, 1970.

Sigonio, Carlo. *De antiquo iure Italiae libri tres ad senatum populumque Romanum.* 2nd ed. Venetiis: Apud Iordanum Ziletum, 1562.

— *Historiarum de regno Italiae libri viginti.* 2 vols. Hanoviae: Typis Wechelianis apud haeredes C. Marnii, 1613.

Simmler, Josias. *De republica Helvetiorum libri duo.* Tiguri: Christophorus Froschoverus, 1576.

Tacitus, G. Cornelius. *De moribus Germanorum.* Ed. Hermann Conring. Helmstedt: Lucius, 1635. Cf. *Dialogus, Agricola, Germania*, trans. William Peterson and Maurice Hutton. Loeb Classical Library. London: Heinemann, 1914.

— *The Histories. The Annals.* Trans. Clifford H. Moore. 4 vols. Loeb Classical Library. London: Heinemann, 1925–1937.

Trithemius, Johannes. *Compendium sive breviarium primi voluminis annalium sive historiarum de origine regum et gentis Francorum.* Parisiis: In officina Christiani Wecheli, sub scuto Basiliensi in vico Iacobaeo, 1539.

— *Chronicon insigne monasterii Hirsaugiensis.* Basileae: Apud Iacobum Parcum, 1559.

Vázquez de Menchaca, Fernando. *Controversiarum illustrium aliarumque usu frequentium libri tres.* Ed. and trans. Fidel Rodriguez Alcalde. 4 vols. Valladolid: Talleres tip. "Cuesta", 1931–1934.

Vitoria, Francisco de. *De Indis et De iure belli relectiones.* The Classics of International Law, ed. J. B. Scott. Washington, DC: Carnegie Institution, 1917.

— *Political Writings.* Ed. and trans. Anthony Pagden and Jeremy Lawrance. Cambridge Texts in the History of Political Thought. Cambridge: Cambridge University Press, 1991.

Warnfried, Paul: *see* Paulus Diaconus.

Westerbergh, Ulla, ed. *Chronicon Salernitanum: A Critical Edition with Studies on Literary and Historical Sources, and on Language.* Acta Universitatis Stockholmiensis. Studia Latina Stockholmiensia 3. Stockholm: Almqvist & Wiksell,

1956. See also "Chronicon Salernitanum," in *Scriptores*, ed. G. H. Pertz, Monumenta Germaniae Historica, 3:470–559. Hannover: Hahn, 1839.

Widukind. "Widukindi res gestae Saxonicae. Die Sachsengeschichte des Widukind von Korvei." In *Quellen zur Geschichte der Sächsischen Kaiserzeit*, ed. and trans. Bauer and Rau, 1–183. See also *PL* 137:123–212. Cf. *The Three Books of the Deeds of the Saxons*, trans. Raymund F. Wood. Ph.D. Diss., University of California, Los Angeles, 1949.

Zosimus. *Historia nova*. 2nd ed. Ed. Fridericus Sylburgius and Christophorus Cellarius. Trans. [from Greek into Latin] Ioannes Leunclavius. Ienae: Krebsianis, 1713. See also *Historia nova*, ed. Ludovicus Mendelssohn. Leipzig: Teubner, 1887. Cf. *Historia nova: The Decline of Rome*, trans. James J. Buchanan and Harold T. Davis. San Antonio: Trinity University Press, 1967; *New History*, trans. Ronald T. Ridley. Byzantina Australiensia 2. Canberra: Australian Association for Byzantine Studies, 1982.

Index

The index contains entries for terms in English and Latin. Where it was easy to combine entries under a single heading because they appeared at the same place in the alphabet (e.g., possession, *possessio*), I have done so. Where it was not easy (e.g., friendship, *amicitia*), I have given separate entries in their respective locations in the alphabet.

abandonment, 21
absolutism, xxvii, xxviii
acclamation, *acclamatio festiva*, 16, 17
Achaeans, *Achaei*, 58, 59
acquisition, *acquisitio*, 10, 11
Adelbert, son of King Berengar, 48, 49, 50, 51, 66, 67
Adelheid, widow of King Lothar, 48, 49
Ado, 30, 31
adoration, *adoratio*, 35, 36, 68, 69; ceremonial, 35, 69; *more antiquorum principum*, 36
Adrianus II, (pope), 24, 26, 34
Adrianus IV, (pope), 74
Aegyptii, 10
Aemilia, 15, 24
Africa, 6, 7, 12, 13
Aistulf, king of the Lombards, *Aistulphus*, 14, 15, 16, 17, 22, 23, 24, 25
Aix-la-Chapelle, 55, 59
Albert, *see* Adelbert

Alcuin, *Albinus*, 26, 27
Alemans, *Alemanni*, 12, 13
Alexander the Great, 76, 77
Alexander III (pope), 62, 63, 64, 65
Alps, *alpes*, 12, 13
Amalasuntha (queen), *Amaleswenta*, 18, 19
America, 6, 7, 79
Americani, 78
amici, 8
amicitia, 30, 32
Amiterno, *Amiternum*, 52, 53
Ammonites, *Ammonitae*, 28, 29
Anastasius Bibliothecarius, 22, 23, 24, 25, 35; *aulae Romanae mancipium*, 24; *vita Hadriani*, 24, 34; *vita Stephani*, 24
Ancona, 15
Ancona (march of), *marcha Anconitana*, 70, 71
Angles, *Angli*, 12, 13, 38, 39
Annales, 30, 32; *see also* Baronio, Cesare

Annales Francici, 22, 24, 26, 30, 34, 36, 42
Annales Francorum, 24
annals, *annales*, 40, 41
anointment, 66
Antichrist, *Antichristus*, 76, 77
Apocalypse, *Apocalypsis*, 76, 77
Apostles, letters of, 77
apostolic see, 69, 71
apostolicae litterae, 76
Apulia, 15
Aquisgranum, 54, 58
archbishops, *archiepiscopi*, 70, 71
Archidamus, *Archidemus*, 28, 29
Archiducatus Austriae, 14
aristocracy, xxvii, xxviii
Aristotelianism, xvi, 90
Aristotle, xi, xxvi, xxvii, xxviii; *Politics*, xiv, xix, xx
Arles, kingdom of, 61, 81
Arnon (river), 28, 29
Arnulf, *Arnolphus*, 46, 47
Asia, 6, 7, 76, 77
assemblies, 53
Assyrians, *Assyri*, 76, 77
auctoritas, 42, 44, 56; *caesarea*, 46, 68; *imperii Romani*, 46; *in pontificem Romanum*, 56; *in populum Romanum*, 56
August, Duke of Brunswick-Wolfenbüttel, xii, xvi, xxi
Augusta Praetoria, *Augusta praetoria*, 30, 31
augustaeum aevum, 78

augustus, 16, 36, 38, 40, 60, 68, 69
Augustus (emperor), xi, 9, 37, 38, 39, 79; age of, 79; *imperator*, 78
aula Romana, 24
Austria, Archduchy of, 15
authority, ix, xxxiv, 43; imperial, 47, 69; of the Roman empire, 47; over bishop and people of Rome, 57
authorship, xiii–xv, xxxiv
autonomy, autonomous, 47, 81
αὐτονομίας, 80
αὔξησιν, 8
Babylon, *Babylonii*, 76, 77
Barlaeus, Caspar, xviii
Baronio, Cesare, xxxv, 22, 23, 24, 25, 26, 27, 28, 29, 34, 35, 40, 41, 44, 45, 48, 49, 50, 51, 52, 53, 66, 67, 68, 69, 70, 71, 72, 73
Bartolus of Sassoferrato, 4, 5, 8, 9
βασιλέα, 32, 33
Batavians, *Batavi*, 6, 9
Bavaria, 63
Bavarians, *Bavari*, 12, 13
Bavarus (elector), 62
Behrens, J., xxv
Belgian-German provinces, *Belgico-Germanicae provinciae*, 54, 55, 58, 59
Belisarius, 14, 15
Bellarmine, Roberto, 36, 37
bellum Hunnicum, 34
Benedict (V, pope), 68, 69
beneficium, 26, 64
Beneventans, *Beneventani*, 30, 31
Benevento, *Beneventum*, 26, 27, 28, 29

Index

Berengar of Friuli, King of Italy, Margrave of Ivrea, *Berengarius dux Foroiuliensis, Eporegiae marchio, rex Italiae*, 48, 49, 50, 51, 66, 67
Beturve, Betuwe, 9
Bible, 9
Biondo, Flavio, 64, 65
bishops, 71
Bodin, Jean, xvi, xxiv, xxv, xxix, 54, 55
Bohemia, 60, 61; king of, 61
Boineburg, Johann Christian von, xii, xv
Boniface VIII (pope), 64, 65
Britain, *Britannia*, 12, 13, 38, 39, 80, 81
brotherhood, 7, 31
Bruno, 70, 71
Brunswick-Wolfenbüttel, Dukes of, x
Burgersdicius, Franco, xviii
Burgundians, *Burgundi*, 12, 13
Burgundy, 61
Busch, J. E., xxv
Byzantine empire, 15
caesar, xxiv, 3, 6, 14, 22, 38, 39, 46, 56, 62, 64, 66, 72, 78; *augustus*, 68, 69; *Constantinopolitanus*, 24, 26; *electus Romani imperii*, 56; *noster*, 80; *qui Constantinopoli degebat*, 14; *Romani imperii*, 56; *Romanus*, 16, 64, 78
caesarea auctoritas, 46, 68; *corona*, 56, 74; *dignitas*, 42, 46, 52; *iura*, 50; *potestas*, 72; *potestas in pontificem populumque Romanum*, 70; *potestas prisca et vera*, 36; *vetus potentia*, 72
caesares, 14, 20, 36, 56, 62, 68, 72, 74, 76; *a Germanis electi*, 56; *Constantinopoli habitantes*, 22; *Constantinopolitani*, 18, 30, 36; *electi*, 56, 74; *Germaniae*, 80; *Germanici*, 74; *Iustiniani successores*, 74; *nostri*, 74, 78; *occidentales*, 38; *prisci*, 62; *qui Constantinopoli commorabantur*, 14; *Romani populi*, 4; *Romanorum*, 14
caesareum nomen, 2, 60, 76, 80
caesareus honor, 42; *titulus*, 40, 48, 56, 68, 80
caesaria tempora, 76
caesarianae partes, 78
Calabria, 14, 15, 16, 17, 30, 31, 66, 67
Calixt, Georg, xvii
Canaan, 10, 11
Canisius, Petrus, 50, 51
Carloman (son of Louis the German), 47
Carolina familia, 46
Carolingian empire, 43; family, 47; law, 55
Carolomannus (son of Louis the German), 46
Carolus IV (emperor), 60
Carolus V (emperor), 60, 78, 82
Carolus Calvus (brother of Lothar, emperor), 44, 58
Carolus Crassus (son of Louis the German, emperor), 46
Carolus Magnus, Carolus, 14, 16, 20, 24, 30, 34, 36, 38, 40, 42, 56, 62, 64, 66, 68, 80; *augustus*, 36, 40; *caesar*, 40; *dominator Frisiorum*, 40; *dominator Saxonum*, 40; *dominus*, 40; *imperator augustus Romanum gubernans imperium*, 40; *nondum imperator*, 34; *patricius Romanus*, 32; *rex*, 26; *rex Francorum et Langobardorum*, 16, 26, 40; *tutor Romani imperii*, 40

Casaubon, Isaac, 73

Caselius, Johannes, xv

Charlemagne, Charles, Charles the Great, 15, 17, 19, 21, 25, 31, 35, 37, 39, 41, 43, 57, 63, 65, 67, 69, 77, 81; adoration of, 37; charters of, 41; conqueror of the Frisians and Saxons, 41; coronation of, xxxiii; daughter of, 29; donation of, 25, 29, 69; election of, 63; emperor and king, 33; Emperor Augustus of the Romans, 17; emperor augustus, 41; Emperor Caesar, 41; governing the Roman empire, 41; guardian of the Roman empire, 41; king of the Franks and Lombards, 17, 27; king of the Franks, 41; letters of, 41; lord, 41; power, 39; power as *patricius*, 37; power over Rome, 35; testament, 37, 41; title, 27, 31, 41

Charles, the Bald (son of Louis the Pious, emperor), 45, 59

Charles, the Fat (son of Louis the German, emperor), 47

Charles IV (emperor), 61

Charles V (emperor), 61, 79, 83

Charles X (king of Sweden), xxi

Chiaramonti, Scipio, xxi

Chinese, 77

Christian world, 55

Christians, *Christiani*, 76, 77

Christina (queen of Sweden), xii, xx

Chronicon Salernitanum, 51

cities, 55; confederated, 9; metropolitan, 37

citizens of Rome, 17, 63, 69

citizenship, 53, 55

cives Romani, 16, 62, 68

civil society, xxvi

civis, 52

civitas, xi, xxv

civitates foedere unitae, 54

civitates Helveticae, 54

claves sancti Petri, 34

codex Iustinianeus, 32

colony, *colonia*, 8, 9

comitatus, 60

comitia, 52

commonwealth. *See* respublica

concilium Nicaenum secundum, 26

confederation, 9, 55, 59

confessio sancti Petri, 34

Conrad (king), 46, 47

Conrad II (emperor), 72, 73

Conring, Hermann, ix; and history, xi; and law, xi–xii; and medicine, x–xi; *De civili prudentia*, ix; *De Germanorum imperio Romano*, xiv–xv, xxx, 53, 77; *De imperii Germanici republica acroamata sex*, xxix–xxx; *De origine iuris Germanici commentarius historicus*, 88; *De politia sive republica in specie sic dicta*, xxv; *Disputatio politica de rebuspublicis in genere*, xxv, xxvii; *Disputatio politica de republica in communi*, xxv; *Exercitatio de imperatore Romano Germanico*, xxxvi; *Exercitatio historico-politica de notitia singularis alicuius reipublicae*, xxv; *Exercitatio politica de optima republica*, xxv; *Exercitationes academicae de republica imperii Germanici*, xxix; his Latin, xxxiii, xxiv; his role as advisor, xii; lectures on the Holy Roman Empire, x, xiv, xv; literature on, 85–94; significance of, ix–xii, xv–xvi; use of italics, xxxiv–xxxv; use of sources, xxx, 7; view of history, xi–xii, xxiii; view of Otto the Great, xxiii; view of the Roman empire, xi; works of, xii, 86

consent, 55, 69

Constantine the Great (emperor), 33

Constantine V Copronymus (emperor), 23

Constantine VI (emperor), 27, 29

Constantinople, *Constantinopolis*, 14, 15, 20, 21, 51; emperor of, 17, 25, 27, 31, 33; emperors of, 15, 19, 21, 23, 33, 37

Constantinopolitans, *Constantinopolitani*, 30, 64, 65

Constantinus (VI, emperor), 26, 28

Constantinus Copronymus (V, emperor), 22

Constantinus Magnus (emperor), 32

constitution, *constitutum*, 78, 79

constitutional government, xxvii–xxviii

consuetudo antiqua, 54; *pristina*, 52

Continuator of Regino, *continuator Reginonis*, 48, 49, 70, 71

contract, *contractus*, 18, 19

corona caesarea, 56, 74; *Germaniae*, 56; *Germanici regni*, 56; *imperii Romani*, 56; *indicium et signum reipublicae*, 54; *Langobardiae*, 56; *regni Germanici*, 54; *regni Teutonici*, 54, 56; *Romana*, 56; *triplex*, 56

coronation, *coronatio*, xxxiii, 54, 55, 56, 64, 65, 69

corpus iuris, 4, 5, 8, 9

corpus legum Romanarum, 78

corpus reipublicae, 38

corpus Sancti Petri, 66

counties, 61

Crancius, Albertus, 40, 68

Crescentius, 70, 71

crown, imperial, 55, 57, 75; of Germany, 55, 57; of Lombardy, 57; of the kingdom, 57; of the Roman empire, 57; of the Teutonic kingdom, 57; Roman, 57; sign or symbol of the state, 55; triple, 57

curia papalis, 72

custom, 55, 61

Dacia, 38, 39

Dalmatia, 30, 31

Danes, *Dani*, 12, 13, 38, 39

Dania, 80

Daniel, 76, 77

Danube, *Danubius*, 6, 7, 16, 17

democracy, xxvii, xxviii

Denmark, xii, 81

derelictio, 20

Descartes, René, xvi

desertores, 50

Desiderius (king of the Lombards), 16, 17, 20, 21, 24, 25, 26, 27, 34, 35

Dietrich of Niem, 70

dignitas, 48, 56, 72, 76, 80; *electoralis*, 62, 63; *imperatoria*, 32, 34, 46, 60; *imperialis*, 42; *imperii*, 44, 64; *imperii occidentalis*, 64; *imperii Romani*, 64; *regia*, 60

dignity, 45, 73, 77, 81; electoral, 63; imperial 33, 35, 43, 47, 49, 53, 57,

61, 65; of the empire, 45; of the Roman empire, 65; of the western empire, 65; royal, 61

Dionysius of Halicarnassus, *Dionysius Halicarnasseus*, 44, 45

diploma, 40, 52, 68; *Caroli Magni*, 40; *donationis*, 70, 72; *Ottonis*, 66; *Ottonis III*, 70, 72

ditio, 14, 16, 50; *Francorum*, 24; *imperii Romani*, 52; *imperii orientalis*, 66; *Langobardorum*, 22; *Romana*, 28, 38; *Romani populi*, 28

divine ordination, 75

doctrina iuris Romani, 78

domination, *dominatus*, 36, 37, 54

dominator, 40

dominium, xxiv, 28; *orbis*, 4, 74; *urbis Romae*, 74

dominus, 18, 40; *orbis*, 74, 78

dominus imperator, 68

donation, *donatio*, 10, 11, 68, 70, 72; *Caroli Magni*, 24; of Charlemagne, 25, 29, 69; of Otto, 67; of Otto III, 71, 73; of Pipin, 25, 29, 69; *Ottonis III*, 70, 72; *Pipini*, 24; *Pipiniana*, 24

ducatus, 26, 28, 60

duces, 50, 68

Duchesne, André, 67

duchy, 15, 61

dukes, 21, 69

dux, 20, 26

East Frisia, xii, xvii

ecclesia Romana, 52, 68

Eginhartus, 30, 32, 36, 40

Egyptians, 11

Einhard, 31, 33, 37, 41

election, *electio*, 56, 57, 62, 63, 68, 74, 75, 82, 83

electors, *electores*, 82, 83

Emilia, 25

Emmanuel (emperor), 64, 65

emperor, 25, 39, 41, 47, 51, 59, 61, 63, 65, 73, 81, 83; elect, 57; lord of the world, 75, 79; of Constantinople, 17, 25, 27, 31, 33; of the Roman empire, 57; old and true power of, 37; *qua* emperor, 59; *qua* king, 59; title of, 3, 57. See also Charlemagne, Roman emperor, Roman empire, Rome

emperors, 29, 47, 57, 75, 77, 81; ancient power of, 63; ancient rights over the pope, 69; eastern, 29, 33; elect, 57, 75; elected by Germans, 57; German, 75, 81; of antiquity, 69; of Constantinople, 15, 19, 21, 23, 33, 37; successors of Justinian, 75

empire, 33, 41, 47, 65, 67, 83; Assyrian, 77; Babylonian, 77; Byzantine, 15; Carolingian, 43; citizenship in, 17, 53, 63, 69; dignity of, 45; eastern, 31, 33, 67; extent, 81; German, 2, 61; literature on, 92; Median, 77; of Charlemagne, 81; of Rome, 77; of the city of Rome, 59, 61; of the Roman people, 57; old, 67; Persian, 77; provinces of, 29; right of, 43; universal, 77; western, 17, 29. See also Charlemagne, *imperium*, Roman empire, Rome

Engelbert, *Engelbertus*, 34, 35

episcopal staff, 71

episcopi, 70

equality, 81

estates, 41, 55

Index

eternity, 77, 79
Europe, *Europa*, 6, 7, 76, 77, 80, 81
evangelium, 8
evidence, 31
exarch, *exarcha*, 20, 21, 34, 35; of Ravenna, 20, 21; power of, 35
exarchalis potestas, 32, 34
exarchate, *exarchatus*, 20, 21, 22, 23; of Ravenna, *Ravennatensis*, 14, 15, 16, 17, 24, 25, 26, 28, 29, 36, 37
facultas creandi regis, 62; *eligendi imperatorem*, 68; *ordinandi summae sedis apostolicae pontificem*, 68
faith, 35
fama, 76
famulatus, 48
Fano, 15
fealty, 51, 67, 69
feuda Germanici imperii, 60
feudum, 48
fidelitas, 66, 68
fides, 34, 48, 50
fiefs, 61
foederati, xxiv; *foederati Helvetii*, 58
foedus, foedera, 30, 58; *aeternum*, 52; *amicitiae*, 32; συμμαχίας, 54
Foroiulienses, 26
France, xii, 27, 39, 43, 45, 59, 81; kingdom of, 41; power of, 77
Franci, 12, 24, 32, 42, 80; *Franci Galli*, 42; *Franci Germaniae*, 42
Francia, 26
Francogalli, 38, 42
Francorum ditio, 24; *libertas*, 42; *potentia*, 32; *regni partitio*, 42; *regnum occidentale*, 58; *regnum orientale*, 58; *regnum*, 42, 44, 58, 76; *rex*, 16, 26, 40; *sedes regni*, 58
Frankish Annals, xxxv, 23, 25, 27, 31, 33, 35, 37, 43
Frankish counts, 27; estates, 41; kingdom, 59; realm, 59; rule, 25
Franks, 13, 27, 37, 41, 43, 81; eastern kingdom of, 59; king of, 17, 27, 41; kingdom of, 41, 43, 45; of Gaul, 43; of Germany, 43; realm of, 77; their custom, 43; their liberty, 43; their power, 33; western kingdom of, 59
fraternitas, 30
fratres Romanorum, 6
Frederick I Barbarossa (emperor), *Fridericus I Barbarossa*, 54, 55, 60, 61, 72, 73, 74, 75
Frederick II (emperor), *Fridericus II*, 60, 61, 72, 73
Frederick III (emperor), *Fridericus III*, 60, 61
free, freedom, 11, 31, 39, 43, 47, 57, 63, 71, 79, 81. *See also* independence, liberty
Freher, Marquard, 71, 72
French, 39, 65
friends, 9
friendship, 31, 33
Frisians, 41
Friuli, 27
Galli, Gallii, 8, 28, 64, 76
Gallia, 12, 16, 38, 42, 44, 58, 80
Gaul, 9, 13, 17, 29
Geoffrey of Viterbo, 59

German emperor, 75, 81; empire, 2, 61; Enlightenment, xv; estates, 55; history, xi–xii, 93; kingdom, 47, 55, 57, 61, 63, 81; kings, 61; language, 81; law, ix, xii; legal history, 89; liberty, 47; magistrates, 39, 59; nationality, 81; nobles, 63; people, 15; peoples, 13, 17; political thought, 89, 90; rights, 81; tribes, 15. *See also* Germany

Germani, 6, 56, 80

Germania, 2, 6, 16, 28, 38, 40, 42, 44, 46, 48, 52, 56, 58, 60, 62, 64, 78, 80, 82; *nostra*, 78

Germaniae caesares, 80; *nomen*, 58; *proceres*, 62; *reges*, 56, 80; *regnum*, 46, 60, 82; *res*, 62; *respublica*, 64; *rex*, 38, 42, 56, 60, 62

Germanic tribes, 15

Germanica respublica, 64

Germanici caesares, 74

Germanici populi, 12, 16

Germanici reges, 60

Germanicum imperium, 2, 60

Germanicum regnum, 46, 52, 54, 56, 60, 62, 80; *caput*, 58; *libertas*, 46; *magistratus*, 58; *ordines*, 54

Germanorum rex, 56, 82

Germans, 57, 65, 81; affairs of, 55, 63; bishops of, 45; boundaries of, xii; crown of, 55, 57; emperors of, 75, 81; head of, 59; history of, xii; honor of, 81; king of, xi, 3, 39, 43, 57, 61, 63, 81, 83; kingdom of, 47, 53, 55, 61, 81, 83; magistrate of, 59; name of, 39, 53

Germany, x, 3, 17, 29, 39, 41, 43, 45, 47, 49, 53, 57, 59, 63, 65, 79, 81; affairs of, 55, 63; bishops of, 45; boundaries of, xii; called Roman empire, 53; crown of, 55, 57; crowned kings of, 57; emperors of, 81; Franks of, 43; head of, 59; history of, xii; honor of, 81; king of (title), 39; kingdom of, 47, 53, 55, 61, 81, 83; kings of, xi, 3, 43, 57, 61, 63, 81, 83; magistrate of, 59; name of, 39; power of, 57; power over, 63

God, 11, 79

Goebel, Johann Wilhelm, xv, xxii, xxix, 86

Gospel, 9

Gotfridus Viterbiensis, 58

Goths, *Gothi*, 12, 13, 18, 19, 38, 39

Graeci, 30, 32

Gratian, *Gratianus*, 52, 53, 68, 69

Greeks, 31, 33, 37

Gregory II (pope), *Gregorius II*, 36, 37

Gregory V (pope), *Gregorius V*, 70, 71

Gregory VII (pope), *Gregorius VII*, 36, 37, 56, 57, 70, 71, 72, 73

Gregory XV (pope), *Gregorius XV*, 62, 63

Grotius, Hugo, xvi; *Apologeticus*, 54, 55; *De antiquitate reipublicae Batavicae*, 8, 9; *De iure belli ac pacis*, xxxvi, 4, 16, 17, 18, 19, 20, 21, 28, 29, 42, 43, 78, 79

Habsburgs, xii

Hadrian II (pope), 25, 27, 35

Hadrian IV (pope), 75

haeresis Henriciana, 72

Harvey, William, x, xvi, 86

Hebrews, *Hebraei*, 10, 11

Helmstedt (university), x, xii
Helvetians, *Helvetii*, 58, 59
Helveticae civitates, 54
Henry I the Fowler (king), *Henricus Auceps*, 46, 47
Henry III (emperor), *Henricus III*, 72, 73
Henry IV (emperor), *Henricus IV*, 36, 37, 52, 53, 70, 71, 72, 73, 82, 83
Henry V (emperor), *Henricus V*, 72, 73
hereditary rights, 47
heresy, 5, 73
Herules, *Heruli*, 14, 15
Herzog August Bibliothek, xvi
Hierosolyma, 60
Hildebrand, *Hildebrandus*, 56, 57
Hincmar of Rheims (archbishop), 44, 45
Hispani, 38, 76
Hispania, 12, 16, 28, 38, 80
Historia Cassinensis, 24
Historia ducum Beneventinorum antiqua, 50
Historia Erphesfordensis, 47
Historia landgraviorum Thuringiae, 46
historiae, 12, 18, 24; *veteres*, 40
historica monumenta, 4
historical records, 25
historical writings, 13
histories, 25
history, x, xi–xii, 19
History of the Landgraves of Thuringia, 47
Histria, 30
Hobbes, Thomas, xvi

Holland, *Hollandia*, 58, 59
Holy Roman Empire, ix, x; Conring's lectures on, x, xiv, xv; literature on, 90, 91. See also Roman empire
honor, *honor*, 42, 43, 68, 69, 71, 80, 81; *caesareus*, 42; imperial, 43; of Germany, 81; title of, 33
Honorius (emperor), 12, 13
Hoym, Bogislaus Otho von, xiii, xiv, xv
Hugh of Arles, *Hugo Arelatensis*, 48, 49
Hungarians, *Hungari*, 14, 15, 38, 39
Hungary, *Hungaria*, 60, 61, 81
Huns, *Hunni*, 13, 14, 35
Iabocus (river), 28
Iephthes, 28
imperator, xxiv, 32, 34, 38, 48, 50, 58, 60, 62, 64, 66, 70, 72, 78; *augustus*, 16, 40, 60; *Constantinopolitanus*, 30, 32; *dominus*, 68; *dominus orbis*, 74; *in quantum est imperator*, 58, 62; *in quantum est rex Germanorum*, 82; *primarius princeps Christiani orbis*, 82; *quatenus rex est*, 58; *Romanorum*, 16, 60; *Romanum gubernans imperium*, 40; *Romanus*, 38, 48, 74; *semper augustus*, 60. See also Roman emperor, Rome
imperatores, 32, 46, 56; *Constantinopolitani*, 16; *Constantinopoli degentes*, 14, 20; *orientales*, 28; *Romanorum*, 14; *Romani*, 20, 56; *Romani electi*, 56
imperatoria dignitas, 32, 34, 46, 60; *potestas*, 74
imperatoris nomen, 32, 38, 44
imperatorium nomen, 58, 72, 74, 80
imperatorius titulus, 20, 28, 36, 40, 46, 60, 76

imperial authority, 47, 69; crown, 75; dignity, 33, 35, 43, 47, 49, 53, 57, 61, 65; honor, 43; legate to St. Peter, 23; name, 73; party, 79; power, 37, 39, 71, 73, 75; precept, 71; rights, 51; title, 21, 29, 33, 37, 39, 41, 45, 47, 49, 57, 59, 61, 69, 75, 77, 81

imperiale praeceptum, 70

imperii amplitudo, 80; *dignitas*, 44, 48, 64; *ditio*, 66; *iura*, 50; *ius*, 10, 42; *nomen*, 58, 62, 80; *reliquae provinciae*, 72; *unctio*, 66

imperii Romani aeternitas, 76; *antiquum cognomentum*, 20; *auctoritas*, 46; *caesar electus*, 56; *cives*, 52; *collatio*, 64; *communis appellatio*, 52; *corona*, 56; *dignitas*, 64; *ditio*, 52; *excidium*, 76; *fines*, 20; *interitus*, 76; *iura in Italia residua*, 22; *ius*, 10, 38; *leges*, 46; *negotia*, 52; *nomen*, 38, 58, 60; *perpetuitas*, 76; *potestas*, 46; *reliqua*, 32; *reliquiae*, 20, 22, 36, 48, 52; *respublicae sociae*, 58; *tutor*, 40; *urbes*, 20

imperium, 32, 40, 46, 82; *amplissimum*, 76; *antiquum*, 72; *Assyriorum*, 76; *Babyloniorum*, 76; *caesaris*, 66; *Caroli Magni*, 80; *Germanici regni*, 80; *Germanicum*, 2, 60; *in Italia*, 20; *Medorum*, 76; *mundi*, 76; *occidentale*, 12, 28, 38, 64, 74; *orientale*, 30, 32, 66, 74; *Persarum*, 76; *Romani populi*, 56; *Romanorum*, 74; *urbis Romae*, 58, 60; *vere dicendum*, 62; *vetus*, 28, 66

imperium Romanum, 2, 16, 38, 40, 42, 44, 46, 48, 56, 58, 60, 62, 64, 74

impietas, 54, 72

independence, independent, xi, xxv, xxvi, xxviii, 13, 25, 47, 49, 81. *See also* freedom, liberty

insula Rheni, 6

interest, 83

investiture, *investitura*, 68, 69

Ioannes (XII, pope), 50, 52, 66, 68

Ioannes (XIII, pope), 70

Ioannes (XV, pope), 70

Iordanes, 18

Iordanus (river), 28

Iornandus, 18

Irene (empress), 26, 27, 28, 29

Isocrates, 28, 29

Istria, 15, 30, 31

Italia, 2, 8, 14, 16, 20, 22, 26, 28, 30, 32, 38, 40, 46, 48, 50, 58, 60, 64, 66, 74, 80; *audiat imperii Romani nomine*, 58; *integra*, 18; *Langobardica*, 38, 42, 64; *universa*, 80

Italiae fines, 18; *optimates*, 48; *proceres*, 50; *reges*, 14, 48, 56; *regnum*, 30, 40, 50, 60, 58, 80; *reliquum*, 64; *respublica*, 64; *rex*, 46

Italy, 3, 9, 15, 17, 19, 21, 23, 27, 29, 31, 33, 39, 41, 47, 49, 59, 65, 67, 75, 81; bishops of, 47; boundaries of, 19, 21, 23; crowned kings of, 57; kingdom of, 27, 41, 51, 53, 55, 59, 61; kings of, 15, 47, 49, 57, 63; Lombard, 39, 43, 59, 65; nobles of, 49, 51; special case of, 19–29

iudices, 68

Iulius Caesar, 6

iura antiqua, 72; *caesarea*, 50; *caesarum*, 68, 74; *imperii*, 50; *in Italia residua*, 22; *in orbem universum*, 76;

maiestatis, 80; *plena*, 80; *positiva*, 78; *quae ante mille annos obtinuerunt*, 78; *rerumpublicarum singularum*, 60; *Romani populi*, 56; *vera et antiqua*, 74; *veterum caesarum in papam*, 68
iuramentum, 52, 66
ius, 28, 30, 32, 60, 72, 76, 78; *ad occupandos Americanos*, 78; *belli*, 6, 10, 24, 38; *caesarum*, 36; *civile*, 10, 18, 20; *creandi summum magistratum Romano imperio*, 56; *deperdita recuperandi*, 28; *divinum arbitrarium*, 10; *eligendi pontificem*, 68; *feudi*, 48, 50; *foederis*, 10; *gentium*, 10; *Germanici regni*, 80; *hereditarium*, 46; *imperii*, 10, 38, 42; *in electionem caesaris*, 62; *in electionem regis Germaniae*, 62; *in Francos*, 42; *in Langobardos*, 42; *in Romanos*, 42; *in urbem Romam*, 32; *integrum*, 80; *naturae*, 10, 18, 20, 78, 82; *occupandi*, 30, 48, 78; *occupationis*, 16; *papae*, 62; *patricii*, 34; *possessionis*, 18, 20, 28, 30; *praescriptionis*, 20; *proprietarium*, 52; *Romani imperii*, 10, 38; *Romanum*, 18, 78; *summum administrandi rempublicam*, 54; *suum*, 12, 46; *usucapionis*, 20; *vis naturalis*, 20
iusiurandum, 66
Iustinianus, 14, 16, 18, 20, 74, 78
Jabbok (river), 29
Jephthah, 29
Jerusalem, 61
John XII (pope), 51, 53, 67, 69
John XIII (pope), 71
John XV (pope), 71
Jordan (river), 29
Jordanes, 19

judges, 69
Judges (book of), 29
Julius Caesar, 7
jurisprudence, ix
Justinian, 15, 17, 19, 21, 63, 75, 79
Justinian Code, 33
king, 59; election of, 63; of Bohemia, 61; of Germany, 63; of the Franks, 17, 27, 41; of the Germans, 57; of the Lombards, 15, 27, 41
kingdom, 55, 83; eastern, of the Franks, 59; elective, 83; hereditary, 83; Italian, 53, 61, 63; of Italy, 27, 41, 51, 53, 55, 59, 61; of Lothar, 47; of the Franks, 59; of the Lombards, 25, 27; of the Romans, 59; western, of the Franks, 59
kingdoms of the Christian world, 55
kings, 75, 77, 83; of Italy, 15, 47, 49, 57, 63; of the Lombards, 15
Knolles, Richard, xxv
Krantz, Albert, 37, 47, 69
Lambert (king of Italy), *Lambertus*, 48, 49
Lampadius, Jacob, x, xi, xviii, xxii, xxv, xxvii, xxviii
Langobardi, 14, 16, 18, 20, 22, 24, 28, 32, 48, 50
Langobardia, 26, 56. *See also* Lombardy, *regnum Langobardicum*
law, ix; Carolingian, 55; civil, 11, 19, 21; divine, 11; eternal, 57; feudal, 49, 51; German, ix, xii; international, xii; natural, xi, xii, 83; natural force of, 21; of God, 11; of nations, 11; of nature, 11, 19, 21, 79; positive, xi, 79;

professors of, 79; public, 89; Roman, xi, xii, 19

laws of Justinian, 63, 75; of the Roman empire, 47; Roman, 79

legates, *legati*, 22, 23, 32, 33, 34, 35, 44, 45, 68, 69, 70, 71

leges imperii Romani, 46; *Iustinianeae*, 62, 74; *Romanae*, 78

legislation, ix

Leibniz, Gottfried Wilhelm, xv, xvi

Leiden, xiii, xiv, xviii

Leo the Isaurian III (emperor), *Leo Isaurus*, 36, 37

Leo V (emperor), 30, 31, 32, 33

Leo III (pope), 16, 17, 34, 35, 36, 37, 68, 69

Leo VIII (pope), 68, 69, 70, 71, 72, 73

Leo of Ostia, *Leo Ostiensis*, 24, 25

Lessing, Gotthold Ephraim, xv, xvi

lex aeterna, 56

lex Carolina, 54

libertas, 14, 44; *Francorum*, 42; *Germanici regni*, 46

liberty, 15, 43, 45, 47, 49, 67, 79

Liburnia, 30, 31

Liguria, 15

Lipsius, Justus, 6, 7

Lithuanians, *Lituani*, 39, 40

Liudprand of Cremona, 51, 67, 69

Locke, John, xvi

Lombard Italy, 39, 43, 59, 65

Lombard kingdom, 21, 23, 29, 31, 33, 37, 43, 47, 49, 51, 53, 57, 59, 61, 63; capital of, 49; in Italy, 49

Lombards, 15, 17, 19, 21, 23, 25, 27, 29, 41, 43; king of, 15, 17, 27, 41; their kingdom, 25, 27, 51

Lombardy, 27, 47, 49, 57; crown of, 57; head of, 59; kingdom of, 53; king of, 27, 57; magistrate of, 59

lord, lordship, xi, 41, 45, 51, 55, 69; of the Christian world, 55; of the city of Rome, 75; of the world, 75, 79; universal, xi

Lothar (king of Italy), 48, 49

Lothar I, (emperor), 42, 43, 44, 45, 47, 58, 59

Lothar III, of Supplinburg, (emperor), 78, 79

Louis the Pious (emperor), *Ludovicus Pius*, 42, 43, 58, 59

Louis of Burgundy (king), *Ludovicus Burgundus*, 48, 49

Louis, son of Louis the German (king), *Ludovicus*, 46, 47

Louis the child (king), *Ludovicus*, 46, 47

Louis the German (king), *Ludovicus*, 44, 45, 46, 47

Louis the Stammerer (king), *Ludovicus Balbus*, 44, 45

Lucas evangelista, 4

Luitprandus Cremonensis, 50, 66, 68, 70

Luke, 5

Luther, Martin, xv

Machiavelli, Niccolò, ix, xvi, xxi

magistracy, magistrate, 3, 39, 57, 59, 75

magistratus, 2; *Germanici regni*, 58; *Langobardici regni*, 58; *Sancti Petri*, 74; *summus*, 38, 56

maiestas, 36, 56, 80
Mainz, archbishop of, xii
majesty, 37
Maximilian (emperor), 60, 61
Medians, *Medi*, 76, 77
medicine, ix, x
Melanchthon, Philip, xv
Messene, *Messena*, 28, 29
Michael (emperor), 30, 31, 32, 33
Migne, Jacques-Paul, xxx
Moeller, Ernst von, 87
Mohammed, 11
monarch, supreme, *monarcha supremus a deo constitutus*, 54, 55
monarchia mundi, 76
monarchy, xxiv, xxvii, xxviii; of the world, 55, 77
monuments, *monumenta*, 24, 40, 41, 52, 53; *antiqua*, 30
mos, 60
Moschi, 38
Muhammed, 10
mundus, 76
Muscovites, 39
Nabuchodonosar, 76
name, empty, 75; imperial, 73; of Germany, 39, 53; of Roman empire, 59, 63. *See also* title
Naples, 15
Narses, 14, 15, 20, 21
nationality, *natio*, 80, 81
natural philosophy, ix
nature, *natura*, 10, 11
Nebuchadnezzar, 77

nefas, 80
Netherlands, x, xvi, 58, 59
Nicaea, second council of, 27
Nicephorus (emperor), 30, 31, 32, 33, 50, 51
Niem, Dietrich of, *Theodoricus de Niem*, 70
Nissen, E., xxv
Nithard, *Nithardus*, 44, 45
nobles, 67
nomen, 38, 78; *augusti et imperatoris caesarisque*, 38; *caesareum*, 2, 60, 76, 80; *caesaris*, 38; *Germaniae*, 58; *Helvetiorum*, 58; *Hollandiae*, 58; *imperatoris*, 32, 38, 44; *imperatorium*, 58, 72, 74, 80; *imperii*, 58, 62, 80; *imperii Romani*, 20, 38, 58, 60; *inane*, 72, 74; *patricii*, 32; *reipublicae Achaeorum*, 58; *sociorum urbis Romanae*, 58
Noricum, *Noricum*, 12, 13, 16, 17
Normans, *Normanni*, 12, 13
Norwegians, *Norvegi*, 12, 13
oath, 53, 67, 69
occident, *occidens*, 28
occupation, *occupatio*, 10, 21, 48
ocean, *oceanus*, 82, 83
Odoacer, 14, 15
οἰκουμένης, 4
oligarchy, xxvii
orbis, 4, 74, 78; *Christianus*, 54, 82; *terrarum*, 2, 4, 8, 10; *totus*, 78; *universus*, 76
ordinatio divina, 74
Ordination of the City of Rome and its Bishops, *ordinatio Romanae urbis et pontificis*, 36, 37

ordo, ordines, 40, 54, 80
Osnabrück, bishop of, 41
Osten, O. J. von, gen. Sacken, xxv
Ostrogoths, *Ostrogothi*, 14, 15, 18, 19
Otgar of Speyer, *Otgarus Spirensis*, 70, 71
Otto I the Great (emperor), xxiii, 46, 47, 48, 49, 50, 51, 52, 53, 56, 57, 62, 64, 65, 66, 67, 69, 70, 71, 72, 73, 80, 81; donation to Pope John, 67; election of, 63; Lord Emperor, 69; oath to Pope John, 53; vassals of, 51
Otto III (emperor), 70, 71
Otto of Freising, *Otto Frisingensis*, 34, 35, 54, 55, 58, 59
Ottonian legend, xxiii
Ottonians, 63
ownership, 19, 53
pact, *pactum*, 30, 31, 66
Pannonia, *Pannonia*, 12, 13, 14, 15, 28, 29, 38, 39
Panvinio, Onofrio, *Onuphrius Panvinius*, 6, 7
papa, 36, 52, 62, 64, 68, 82; *civis alicuius reipublicae*, 52; *monarcha supremus*, 54; *Romanus*, 22, 52, 56, 62, 64, 74. See also pontifex
papacy, 57, 63, 75
Papia, 26, 50, 56; *metropolitana urbs*, 48; *sedes regia*, 48
Paracelsus, x, 86
Paris, 27
patriciate, *patriciatus*, 33, 34, 35
patricius, 33, 34, 35, 36, 37; *Romanus*, 32
patrimonium, 28; *papae*, 36; *Petri*, 16, 36, 72; *pontificis*, 32

patrimony, 29; of the pope, 33, 37; of St. Peter, 17, 73
patrocinium, 28
Paul IV (pope), 62, 63
Paul Warnfried (Paul the Deacon), *Paulus Warnefridus*, 18, 19
Pavia, 27, 49, 51, 57
pax, 48
Peace of Westphalia, x
pedum episcopale, 70
Pentapolis, 14, 15, 16, 17, 24, 25
perpetuitas, 76
Persian empire, 77
Persians, *Persae*, 76, 77
Perugia, 15
Pesaro, 15
Peter (Saint), 17, 23, 35, 37, 67, 75
Petri corpus, 66; *patrimonium*, 72; *preces et impie confictae litterae*, 22
Petronius, 4, 5
Pipin (king), *Pipinus*, 16, 22, 23, 24, 25, 28, 30, 31, 68; donation of, 29, 69; king of the Franks, 17
Pipin (son of Charlemagne), *Pipinus*, 26, 27
Pithou, Pierre, *Pithoeus*, 40, 41
Platina, Bartolomeo, 64, 65
plebs Romana, 70
Pliny, *Plinius*, 8, 9
Poch, G., xxv, xxvii
Poeta Saxo, 26, 27
Poland, 81
Poles, 39
polis, xi

politics, ix, 89, 90
polity, xxvii
Poloni, 38
Polonia, 80
pomoerium, 14
pontifex, 32, 66, 68, 70, 72, 78; *Romanus*, 16, 24, 26, 28, 36, 48, 56, 70, 74; *summae sedis apostolicae*, 68
pontificatus, 34
pontifices, 74, 80; *gloriosissimi et superbissimi nebulones*, 80; *Romani*, 64, 70; *Romanorum*, 56
pope, 37, 41, 53, 63, 65, 67, 69, 71, 73, 75, 81, 83; as citizen, 53, 55; patrimony of, 33, 37; Roman, 23, 53, 57, 63, 65, 75; said to be God, 79; supreme monarch, 55
populi sui iuris, 12; *foederati*, 8; *septentrionales*, 38
populus Romanus, 4, 10, 12, 14, 16, 18, 24, 26, 28, 34, 38, 48, 54, 56, 64, 70, 78
possessio, 10, 20, 28, 30, 32, 38, 48, 52, 74; *privata*, 28, 82; *publica*, 28; *quieta*, 80. *See also* ius
possession, 11, 19, 29, 31, 33, 53, 75, 81; private, 29, 83; public, 29; rightful, 21
possessions, 11, 13, 17, 29, 31
possessors, *possessores*, 18, 19
potentia, 72; *caesarea*, 72; *Francorum*, 32; *Gallorum*, 76; *Hispanorum*, 76; *in populum Romanum*, 56; *pristina et iusta caesarum*, 72; *vasta*, 76; *vetus*, 72
potestas, 32, 44, 48, 50, 54, 66, 70; *caesarea*, 36, 72; *caesaris nostri*, 80;

caesarum, 36, 62; *creandi caesarem*, 62; *eligendi caesarem*, 62; *eligendi imperatores*, 56; *exarchalis*, 32, 34; *Germanorum*, 56; *imperatoria*, 74; *imperii Romani*, 46; *in imperatorem*, 72; *in liberas respublicas*, 80; *in pontificem Romanum*, 70; *in populum Romanum*, 70; *in principes*, 72; *in reges*, 72; *in urbem Romam*, 34; *Ottonis Magni*, 48; *patricii*, 36; *prisca et vera caesarea*, 36; *priscorum caesarum*, 62; *summa*, xxviii, 54; *suprema*, 66; *urbis Romae*, 74
power, 49, 81; imperial, 37, 39, 71, 73, 75, 81; of ancient emperors, 63; of Berengar, 49, 51; of Charlemagne, 35, 37, 39, 67; of France, 77; of Franks, 33; of Germans, 57; of Lombards, 15; of Lothar's brothers, 45; of Ostrogoths, 15; of Otto, 67; of *patricius*, 37; of Spain, 77; of the exarch, 35; of the pope, 73; of the Roman empire, 47; old and true, 37; old imperial, 73; over emperors, 73; over Germany, 63; over Italy, 33; over Rome, 35; over the bishop and people of Rome, 57, 71; over the city of Rome, 35, 37, 75; over the pope, 37; sovereign, 55; supreme, 67; to choose kings of Germany and Italy, 63; to elect the emperor, 57, 63
praefectus praetorio, 20
praerogativa, 76
praescriptio longi temporis, 16, 20, 28, 74
Praetorian Prefect, 21
precedence, 81
prerogative, 77
prescription, 17, 21, 29, 75

primogeniture, *primogenitura*, 42, 43
primogenitus, 44
prince, princes, 37, 55, 61, 73, 83
princeps, 54, 60; *primarius Christiani orbis*, 82
principatus, 70
principes, 72; *antiqui*, 36
principia natura nota, 10
private, 29, 83
Privilegium Osnabrugensis episcopatus, 40
proceres civitatis, 66; *Germaniae*, 62; *Italiae*, 50; *regni Langobardici*, 50
προεδρία, 80
property, 29. See also ownership, possession
Protestant Reformation, xv
provinces, 9, 17, 19, 21, 27, 29, 31, 39, 61, 73; united Belgian-German, 55
provinciae, 6, 8, 16, 18, 26, 28, 30, 38, 60, 72; *foederatae Belgico-Germanicae*, 54, 58; *Romani imperii in Italia*, 20
public, 29
Pufendorf, Samuel von, ix, xvi
Puteanus, Erycius, *Eyricius Puteanus*, 20, 21
Pyrenees, *Pyrenaei montes*, 12, 13, 38, 39
Raetia, 13, 17
Ragusa, xxix, 81
Ravenna, 14, 15, 16, 17, 20, 22, 23, 24, 25, 26, 28, 29, 36, 37. See also exarchate
realm, 59, 77
Reate, 52
rebels, *rebelles*, 50, 51, 72
rebellion, *rebellio*, 36, 37, 73

regalia, *regalia*, 74, 75
reges, 18, 42, 46, 56, 60, 72, 76; *Germaniae*, 2, 56, 80; *Germanici*, 60; *Italiae*, 14, 46, 48, 56; *Langobardorum*, 14, 56; *nostri*, 54, 74; *Ostrogothorum*, 14
Regino of Prüm, 68, 69
regna, 54, 60; *orbis Christiani*, 54; *vastissima*, 76
regnum, xxviii, xxix; *Arelatense*, 60, 80; *Burgundicum*, 60; *electitium*, 82; *Franciae*, 40; *Francicum*, 40, 58; *Francorum*, 42, 44, 58, 76; *Francorum Gallorum*, 42; *Francorum Germaniae*, 42; *Germaniae*, 60, 82; *Germanicum*, 46, 56; *hereditarium*, 82; *Italiae*, 40, 50, 60; *Italicum*, 50, 52, 54, 60, 62; *Italicum Langobardorum*, 48; *Langobardicum*, 22, 28, 30, 36, 42, 46, 48, 50, 52, 56, 60, 62; *Langobardicum Italiae*, 58; *Langobardorum*, 20, 24, 26, 32, 50; *Lotharii*, 46, 58; *occidentale*, 58; *orientale*, 58; *Persarum*, 76; *Romanorum*, 60; *Sarracenorum*, 76; *Sinensium*, 76; *Tartarorum*, 76; *Turcarum*, 76
reipublicae orbis Christiani, 54
religion, ix
republics of the Christian world, 55
respublica, xi, xxiv, 52, 54, 56, 60, 72, 78, 80; *Achaeorum*, 58; *corpus*, 38; definition of, xxiv–xxix; *Germaniae*, 64; *Germanica*, 54; *Italiae*, 64; *libera*, 48, 78, 80; *magna*, 80; *natura*, 60; *nostra*, 78; *parva*, 80; *Rhegusina*, 80; *Romana*, 2; *sui iuris*, 46
respublicae, 58, 78; *coniunctae*, 60; *distinctae*, 62; *liberae*, 80; *orbis Christiani*, 54; *sociae Romani imperii*, 58

reverence, *reverentia*, 42, 43, 46, 47
rex, 16; *Ammonitarum*, 28; *Bohemiae*, 60; *Francorum*, 26; *Germaniae*, 42, 56; *Germanorum*, 82; *Hungariae*, 60; *Italiae*, 46; *Langobardiae*, 26; *Langobardorum*, 26
Rhenus, 6, 12, 16
Rhetia, 12, 16
Rhine, 7, 9, 13, 17
Rhône, *Rhodanus*, 38, 39, 80, 81
Rieti, 53
right, 75; divine, 11; of conquest, 7; of empire, 43; of occupation, 11, 17, 31, 49; of ownership, 19, 53; of possession, 29, 31; of prescription, 21; of recovering losses, 29; of usucapion, 21; of war, 11, 25, 39; sovereign, 55; to elect emperor, 63; to elect kings of Germany and Italy, 63; to occupy America, 79; to rule Italy, 33; to the city of Rome, 33; to rule the world, xi, 11
rights, 11, 81; ancient, 69, 73, 75; hereditary, 47; loss of, 11; of emperors, 75; of sovereignty, 81; of the German emperor, 81; of the Roman empire, 3, 23; of the Roman emperor, 79; of the Roman people, 29, 57, 79; over the pope, 69; over the world, 77; true, 75
Rimini, 15
Rodulfus Glaber, *Rodulphus Glaber*, 70, 71
Roma, 26, 34, 36, 70, 72, 74; *excidium*, 76; *sedes apostolica*, 70; *urbs*, 10, 22, 36, 72; *vexillum*, 34
Roman archives, 25; bishop, 25, 27, 57, 65, 75; bishopric, 67; Church, 53, 69; citizens, 63; court, 25; crown, 57; imperial title, 49, 57; laws, 79; Patricians, 35; people, 11, 15, 19, 25, 27, 29, 39, 55, 57, 59, 71; pope, 23, 53, 57, 63, 65, 75; right to rule the world, xi, 11; rule, 29, 39
Roman emperor, xi, 15, 21, 39, 49, 57, 65, 67, 61, 71, 75
Roman empire, xi, 3, 21, 23, 39, 43, 45, 47, 49, 53, 57, 59, 61, 63, 75; as name of Germany, 39; authority of, 47; boundaries of, 21; destruction of, 77; dignity of, 65; eastern, 13, 75; eternity of, 75, 77; highest magistrate of, 57; laws of, 47; name of, 59, 63; power of, 47; provinces in Italy, 21; remaining rights in Italy, 23; remnants in Italy, 23; remnants of, 37, 49, 53; rights of, 3, 29, 57, 59; rule of, 53; translation of, 37; universal, 3, 5; western, 13, 27, 29, 37, 39, 75
Romani, 20, 28, 32, 34, 42, 56; *cives*, 68; *pontifices*, 64, 70
Romanorum caesares, 14; *Imperator Augustus*, 16; *imperator semper augustus*, 60; *imperatores*, 14, 70; *imperatorum legati*, 70; *pontifices*, 56
Romans, 21, 29, 33, 35, 43, 57, 61
Romanum imperium, 2, 16, 38, 40, 42, 44, 46, 48, 56, 58, 60, 62, 64, 74
Romanus imperator, 38, 48, 74
Romanus papa, 22, 52, 56, 62, 64, 74
Romanus pontifex, 16, 24, 26, 28, 36, 48, 56, 70, 74
Romanus populus, 4, 10, 12, 14, 16, 18, 24, 26, 28, 34, 38, 48, 54, 56, 64, 70, 78

Rome, xi, 23, 25, 27, 33, 35, 37, 71, 73; allies of, 59; bishop of, 17, 29, 49, 57, 71; citizens of, 17, 63, 69; city of, 11, 15, 21, 29, 35, 37, 59, 61, 73, 75, 77; destruction of, 77; duchy of, 15; emperor of, 17, 79; empire of, 77; magistracies of, 75; people of, 17, 35, 39, 49, 57, 65, 71, 79; regalia of, 75; standard of, 35

Rotgaud (duke of Friuli), *Rotgaudus dux*, 26, 27

Rotrud (daughter of Charlemagne), 28, 29

Rudolph of Burgundy, *Rudolphus Burgundus*, 48, 49

S. *Petrus*, 16, 22, 24, 66

Sacred Scripture, *sacrae litterae*, 11, 74, 75, 76, 77

St. Peter, 17, 23, 35, 37, 67, 73, 75

St. Vincent (monastery), 26, 27

Saracens, *Sarraceni*, 76, 77

Savigny, Friedrich Karl von, 87

Saxon Poet, *Poeta Saxo*, 26, 27

Saxons, *Saxones*, 12, 13, 40, 41

Saxony, *Saxonia*, 70, 71

Scaliger, Joseph Justus, 20, 21

sceptre, *sceptrum*, 50, 51

Schwyz, 59

science, ix

Scots, *Scoti*, 38, 39

Seifert, Arno, xxiii

septentrionales populi, 38

Sicily, *Sicilia*, 60, 61

Sigismund (emperor), 60, 61

Sigonio, Carlo, *Sigonius*, 8, 9, 30, 31, 46, 47

Simmler, Josias, *Iosias Simlerus*, 54, 55

Sinenses, 76

Sinigaglia, 15

societas, 6, 32

socii, 8

somnium Danielis, 76

somnium Nabuchodonosaris, 76

sovereignty, xi, xxvi, xxviii, xxix, 55, 57, 81

Spain, 13, 17, 29, 39, 77, 81

Spaniards, 39

Spoleto (duchy), 27

state, states, xi, xxix, 47, 49, 53, 55, 57, 59, 63, 65, 79, 81; affairs of, 53; definition of, xi; free, 79; literature on, 92, 93; nature of, 61; of Europe, ix; separate, 59; sign or symbol of, 55

statistics, ix

Stephen (pope), *Stephanus papa*, 22, 23, 24, 25, 34, 35

Stobbe, Otto, 87

Stockholm, xii

Stolleis, Michael, 85, 86, 89

subditi, 8

subjection, *subiectio*, 34, 35

subjects, 9

Sueci, 38

Suevi, 12

sui iuris, 12, 46

summa potestas, xxviii, 54

συμμαχίας, 54

Svecia, 80

Svevicus ducatus, 60
Sviceri, 58
Swabia (duchy), 61
Swabians, 13
Sweden, xii, 81
Swedes, 39
Swiss cities, 55
Sylvester II (pope), 70, 71
tablets, *tabulae*, 52, 53
Tacitus, xiv, 6, 7, 8
Tatars, *Tartari*, 77
testamentum Carolinum, 36, 40
testimonium, 24, 26, 80
Teutonic kingdom, 57
Thebans, *Thebani*, 28, 29
Theodoric (king), *Theodoricus*, 14, 15
Theodosius (emperor), 12, 13
Theophanu (empress), *Theophane*, 72, 73
title, 3, 11, 39, 41, 61, 57; imperial, 3, 49, 57, 81; of Burgundy, 61; of Charlemagne, 27, 31, 41; of Charles IV, 61; of Frederick III, 61; of honor, 33; of Jerusalem, 61; of Sigismund, 61; to Italy, 19
titulus, 10, 26, 38, 60, 74; *acquirendi*, 10; *Arelatensis regni*, 60; *Burgundici regni*, 60; *caesareus*, 40, 48, 56, 68, 80; *Caroli IV.*, 60; *Caroli Magni*, 28, 30, 40; *dignitatis*, 32; *Hierosolymae*, 60; *imperatoris*, 2, 28, 32, 38, 40; *imperatorius*, 20, 28, 36, 40, 46, 60, 76; *inanis*, 30; *Italici regni*, 60; *possidendi*, 10; *regis Germaniae*, 38, 60; *regni Francici*, 40; *regni Langobardici*, 40; *regum Germaniae*, 56;

Romanorum imperatoris, 2; *Siciliae*, 60; *solus*, 32; *Svevici ducatus*, 60
tradition, *traditio*, 10
Trajan (emperor), *Traianus*, 6, 7
treaty, 11, 31, 33, 55, 67
Trithemius, Johannes, 42, 43, 44, 45
Turks, *Turca*, 74, 75, 76, 77
tyranny, *tyrannis*, xxv, 50, 70, 51, 71
unctio, 66
Ungaria, 80
University of Helmstedt, ix, xvii
University of Leiden, ix, xviii
urbes, 20, 36, 70
urbs, 8, 10, 70; *Roma*, 14, 20, 28, 32, 34, 36, 72, 74; *Romana*, 10, 22, 36, 58, 72, 76; *Veneta*, 14, 22, 66
usucapion, *usucapio*, 16, 17, 20, 21
usura, 82
Valentinian III (emperor), *Valentinianus*, 12, 13
Vasquius, Ferdinandus, 20, 78
vassals, 51
Vatican Library, *Vaticana bibliotheca*, 24, 25
Vázquez, Ferdinand, 21, 79
Veneta urbs, 14, 22, 66
Veneti, 30, 66
Venetia, 14
Venetiae, 14, 30
Venetians, 31, 67
Venice, 15, 23, 31, 67
veritas aeterna, 78
vexillum Romanae urbis, 34
Vindelicia, 12, 13, 16, 17

violentia, 72

vis, 38, 56, 74, 80

Vitoria, Francisco de, *Victoria*, 78, 79

Waal, 9

west, *occidens*, 28

Westphalia, Peace of, xii, xvi, 87

Widukind of Corvey, *Witichindus, Witikindus*, 48, 49

Wieacker, Franz, 89

world, xi, 11, 75, 77, 79; Christian, 55, 83; end of, 75, 77; lord of, 79

world monarchy, 77

Zeno, 18, 19

Zonaras, 37

Zosimus, 32, 33